P9-DMZ-267

The Muse in the Machine

The Life of Poetry Poets on Their Art and Craft

The **Muse** in the Machine

Essays on Poetry
and the Anatomy of
the Body Politic

by T. R. Hummer

The University of Georgia Press

Athens & London

© 2006 by The University of Georgia Press
Athens, Georgia 30602
All rights reserved
Designed and typeset by Louise OFarrell
Set in 9.8/14 Scala
Printed and bound by Maple-Vail
The paper in this book meets the guidelines for
permanence and durability of the Committee on
Production Guidelines for Book Longevity of the
Council on Library Resources.

Printed in the United States of America

10   09   08   07   06   c   5   4   3   2   1
10   09   08   07   06   p   5   4   3   2   1

Library of Congress Cataloging-in-Publication Data

Hummer, T. R.
The muse in the machine : essays on poetry and the
anatomy of the body politic / by T. R. Hummer.
        p.   cm. — (Life of poetry)
Includes bibliographical references (p.   ) and index.
ISBN-13: 978-0-8203-2803-4 (alk. paper)
ISBN-10: 0-8203-2803-0 (alk. paper)
ISBN-13: 978-0-8203-2797-6 (pbk. : alk. paper)
ISBN-10: 0-8203-2797-2 (pbk. : alk. paper)
    1. American poetry—20th century—History and criticism.
2. Politics and literature—United States—History—20th
century. 3. Literature and society—United States—History—
20th century. 4. Poetry—Authorship. I. Title. II. Series.
PS323.5H86 2006
811'.509358—dc22   2005031543

British Library Cataloging-in-Publication Data available

Contents

Acknowledgments

"An Audience": An initial, much shorter version of this essay was published in the Hawaiian literary journal *Manoa*, but the piece grew over the years. In 2003 the final form of it was delivered as a keynote speech at Humanities Washington's annual Humanities Awards Luncheon in Seattle; it is posted on their web site at http:// www.humanities.org.

"Laughed Off: Canon, *Kharakter*, and the Dismissal of Vachel Lindsay" was originally published in *The Kenyon Review*, Winter 1994.

"'Sen-Sen,' Censorship, Obscenity, Secrecy: Slapping the Face of the Body Politic": An excerpted version of this essay appeared in the *AWP Chronicle* and the whole piece in *New England Review*, Fall 1991.

"Inside the Avalanche" first appeared in *What Will Suffice: Contemporary American Poets on the Art of Poetry*, edited by Christopher Buckley and Christopher Merrill (Salt Lake City: Gibbs-Smith, 1995).

"Ex Machina: Reading the Mind of the South" was previously published in *The Southern Review*, Winter 1996.

"Revenge of the American Leviathan" was previously published in *New England Review*, Spring/Summer 1992.

"'Christ, Start Again': Robert Penn Warren, a Poet of the South?" was published in *The Legacy of Robert Penn Warren*, edited by David Madden (Baton Rouge: Louisiana State University Press, 2000).

"The Mechanical Muse": The full essay was published under the title "Tutelary Instruments" in Fall 2003 in the electronic journal *Blackbird*, available on the web at http://www.blackbird.vcu.edu. A short version under the present title appeared in *The Oxford American* (Sixth Annual Music Issue, April 2003) and was chosen by Mickey Hart of The Grateful Dead for inclusion in the anthology *Best Music Writing* for 2004 (New York: Da Capo, 2004).

Introduction

This is a book born of trouble: a troubled mind, a troubled art, troubled times. I am tempted to say *my* mind, *my* art, *my* times, but to say so would be at best a half truth, because the trouble I'm talking about was and is far from only mine.

The essays assembled here were not originally written to be a book, but since they all emanate from the desk of one obsessive worrier, they are shot through with similar concerns: the soul of American poetry, the nature of the American body politic, the definition of conscience, the cost of racism, the ameliorative potential—if not actually redemptive power—of art. The oldest of these was published well over a decade ago, the newest in 2004. Some are about subjects that are persistent if not actually timeless; others concern themselves with cultural moments that, on the surface, look ephemeral—the collapse of the poet Vachel Lindsay, the Salmon Rushdie affair, a scandal at the National Endowment for the Arts. But all these matters are, as William Carlos Williams would say, in the American grain, and our current situation has reawakened me to their relevance. If I have faith in these essays at this remove, it is not because of the writing that is mine but because of the trouble that is not.

Still, my own trouble is my starting point; it is also my impetus. It is fair to begin there.

In the late 1980s I came to a crisis point simultaneously in my mental life and in my art. A certain way of writing poems, which I had labored for years to master, suddenly played out for me, and I was struggling to reinvent myself as a poet. Years of working as a literary editor—*Quarterly West, Cimarron Review, Kenyon Review,* and by 1990 *New England Review*—had wrought in me an increasingly public awareness of the nature and role of literary writing. And things were going on in the nation—the endgame of the Reagan-Bush years—that I was finding increasingly unbearable. I was troubled, then, and so found everything else troubling.

Make no mistake: I am not talking about depression—personal, clinical, chemical, situational, or however defined. No group therapy, twelve-step program, or bottle of Prozac, with all due respect to those agencies, was going to help. I am talking about cultural challenge. I am talking, too—curiously enough, since I was in my early forties—about coming to a certain kind of maturity, which maybe in our culture involves arriving at middle age, wherein I felt responsible for the world in which I found myself: part of the mechanism, not just a passenger on a speeding train. Increasingly I experienced the world as *my* world, in a guilty sense. Circumstance forced me to admit it: *These things of darkness I acknowledge mine.*

Years before, in the winter of 1987, I had begun writing what I soon discovered would be a long poem. I began it with joy and in a spirit of playfulness; but it rapidly tried to take me into territory previously uncharted, at least by me, and I found that I was unequipped to go there. Always studious, I read harder, thought harder, grew older. The poem I had begun—like a hurricane with its attendant tornadoes—spawned a front of smaller poems, mostly dark and turbulent ones. The shorter poems taught me little lessons about the long one; the stormy season endured.

And then, on January 16, 1991, George H. W. Bush took the nation into Iraq.

My response was, in retrospect, predictable: I was in shock briefly, and then I began to write. I wrote more short poems, and the long poem that was the dark dynamo behind them took shape and finished itself: "Walt Whitman in Hell," a mere ten pages, four years in the making.

I wrote other things as well, mostly essays: editorials for *New England Review*, pieces for any journal that would take them. This process was as much about clarifying my own thinking as it was about making public statements, but being public was indispensable. I was haunted by a pervasive sense of culpability, which was both personal and collective. Everything I had learned about human character told me that war is with us always, but the lessons of Vietnam, and the prevailing public backlash in the wake of that conflict, had left me with a subliminal, naïve conviction that it would never happen again. That illusion was shattered. I wrote beyond myself, driven by images of America bombed and burning—as if every time we dropped ordnance on Baghdad, an equal and opposite spiritual bomb fell here:

Friendly Fire
Land war will require the most complex
combat flying ever flown, with more
tragedies of friendly fire inevitable.
                        —CNN newscast, 2/4/91

Heraclitean, for instance: the world as a gaseous
Shimmer, like afterburner fumes in the oily night sky
Outside Carbondale, where lovers pass through the flux
Of the heart's napalm—or alchemical: the transformative image
Of the sun over Dallas, antiseptic if you could touch it,
Tritely ætherial, the volatile gold of gas-well burn-off
On the freeway's horizon, cauterizing, uncorrupting bone—

We could imagine anything. Suppose we pulled a lever
And every carburetor in Charlottesville
Detonated in a transcendental rush of mustard gas
And oxyacetylene? What would we think we were seeing?
What residue would remain?
                                        I think it would be elemental.
I think it would be pure. I think it would give off the smell
Of brass, chrysanthemum, caustic old velour—
Or that strange metallic odor that drags my grandmother's face
Up from the flare of my neurons, where the innocent dead all go:
A bombed-out country no body belongs to, untouchable, chemical,
      clean.

And then the storm passed. The United States pulled out of Iraq;
Bush lost the election; Al Gore invented the Internet. We entered a
time that was, on the surface, far less troubled. I left the profession
of editing; moved to Oregon; played jazz; ate well; moved to Richmond, Virginia; played blues; remarried; had a child; moved to
Georgia; re-entered the profession of editing. And suddenly, it was
September 2001.

   In retrospect, it is clear that the events of the early 1990s were no
more than harbingers; the real trouble lay in the not-too-distant future that has an insidious way of suddenly becoming the present.
Near the end of the twentieth century, I had looked over the essays
I had written at that time with the intention of making a book of
them; but in the silicon glow of the Clinton years, much that I found
there seemed irrelevant, and I put the idea aside. Then, after September 11, 2001, I found myself going back—first to the poems I
had written during that time, such as "Friendly Fire." The image of
America burning was now no mere metaphor; the equal but opposite bombs that had fallen on us, and seemed sure to fall again, were
not spiritual but material and immediate.

   One section of "Walt Whitman in Hell" kept whispering in
my ear. Near the end of the poem, Whitman's ghost, having made a

long journey through the underworld of the New York subway system, re-emerges at the foot of the Brooklyn Bridge, where he finds that

> Nothing has changed. Manhattan grinds on,
> Gears of the living irreversibly meshed
>
> With the ratchet of desire. There is still the apocalyptic
> Discharge of cluster-bombs over the lower east side,
> Brimstone of artillery out of the Village, sniper fire
>
> From the Chrysler Building, the strafing
> Of Bloomingdales. But everything on the earth I love
> Is sealed from my touch as by a zone
>
> Of Platonic plate glass. In my loneliness I rise
> And hover over the plutonium-gray span
> Of East River, licked by the harrowing fallout
>
> Of my own intangibility. From here I can see,
> Like a skyline, the obvious contour of all
> My error. O I freely confess it now: America,
>
> I was wrong. I am only slightly larger than life.
> I contain mere conspiracies. What do I know?
> There is no identity at the basis of things, no one
>
> Name beneath all names. There is no more than this
> To remember: *It is not godlike to die. It is not even human.*
> *Refuse the honor, no matter who tells you its conquest is sublime.*

Just before emerging into war-torn, burning Manhattan, this Whitman has a vision of himself as the President of the Dead,

> Commanding rank and file of the husks
> Of riveters and lawyers (I gathered them
> Tenderly as they settled), and residues of secretaries,

Dregs of ushers, gynecologists, thieves,
And the fine ash of Iraqi cabdrivers,
And the delicate grit of Marines,

Dust of Bush, Baker, Schwarzkopf, Cheney,
And beautiful Colin Powell: such a clay they made,
Such a multitude molded, such drum-taps and battle hymns.

At last I believed I understood them. At last
When I called their names they seemed
To shiver to hear me, as if they were almost alive.

A few years after the poem was published, I came to regret
that catalog of names—Bush, Baker, Schwartzkopf, Cheney, Colin
Powell. My model for including them was William Blake, within
whose long poems one can find lengthy catalogs, usually in a vitriolic
context, of the names of political figures now completely obscure;
but during the Clinton presidency, I began to think "Baker? Cheney?
Powell? Who will remember these figures in ten years?" I now have
been reminded that the power of the repressed to return is infinite,
and that certain patterns in the human world are well-nigh ineradicable.

The materials out of which this work is made are American
materials, human materials, not my personal substance: "[T]he fine
ash of Iraqi cabdrivers, / And the delicate grit of Marines." It is
to these materials that this work is owed, and to which I dedicate it
now.

T. R. Hummer, September 2004

An Audience

> [T]he poetic audience, even among
> intellectuals, has largely vanished.
> —Christopher Clausen

> [T]here are three to four times as
> many books of poems published now
> as there were in 1940 . . . and the
> print-orders of books published by
> major publishers are five to ten times
> greater than they were.
> —Donald Hall

This begins, like so many things, with a mistake I made. In the fall of 1990, I was interviewed by a reporter from the *Burlington (Vermont) Free Press* who was writing a piece about plans for *New England Review*, the literary quarterly of which I had recently become the editor. We talked for a while about *NER*'s editorial policies and procedures—how many manuscripts arrived daily in the mail (fifty), how many ultimately saw print, all the usual questions. The conversation focused mainly on the pragmatics of our internal operations, so it is perhaps understandable that when she innocently asked, "And how many readers do you have?" I replied, with equal innocence, "Oh, there are only the two of us."

In the shocked silence that followed my answer, I had the obvious epiphany—that my interrogator had made a transition in her questioning that I had not followed. She meant, of course, for me to tell her the size of *New England Review*'s audience; I thought she wanted to know how many editors screened the incoming manuscripts.

At the time, the momentary misunderstanding was first confusing, then comic. But in retrospect I realize that it is also instructive. The fact that the word *reader* applies equally to editor and audience is no accident; this sameness indicates a connection that sometimes gets lost in the shuffle when we talk about the complicated set of relationships among writer, reader, text, and editor.

How must it have sounded, at first blush, to the friendly *Free Press* reporter—herself, of course, a writer, one immediately responsible to an editor and to a sizable readership—when my reply to her question turned out to be not merely *two*, a figure ridiculous enough in itself, but "only the two *of us*"? How often has it been said by critics and by the public at large—not to say by the sort of "hard-nosed professional writer" a reporter stereotypically is—that poetry and "literary" fiction are highly rarefied enterprises, and that, for instance, poets write only for other poets? How much more shocking is the idea that a couple of editors out in the Vermont hinterland might be producing a hefty, handsome literary magazine for the consumption of "only the two of us"? How could we possibly justify our parasitic existence?

The very idea is comic. And yet it remained true that *New England Review*'s relatively small circulation—twenty-five hundred or so at that point—was paltry by comparison even with that of the *Burlington Free Press*, just as sales of my last book of poems were paltry by comparison with the circulation of *USA Today*. And it is also true that, when I justified *New England Review*'s budget to the Middlebury College accountant, as every year I had to do, it became clear that the figure of twenty-five hundred sounded to him not so different from "only the two of us."

"A readership cannot be judged simply on the basis of a number," I find myself saying over and over. And I am correct every single time I say it. Yet the beat goes on. It is a familiar beat as monotonous as disco, and it says, "Who do you think you are, you poets, you fiction writers, you artists, you editors of lit mags, you parasites, you who produce no junk bonds and drive no BMWs? For whom do you write? For whom do you publish? Where's the dividend?"

We've heard all that, again and again. We've heard it from accountants, who are, it must be said, generally good and responsible people; we've heard it in a different key from the likes of Jesse Helms and Patrick Buchanan, whom I for one am not prepared to call *good* or *responsible*, but who make a difference when they say it. To those "of us" in the field, it grows tedious. But in all honesty we ought to remember that this sort of question does have its basis in a very real knot of complicated issues that have no obvious solutions. Why should the general public, whatever that awful phrase may mean, *not* have doubts about the poet, the "literary" fiction writer, the lit mag editor?

At the heart of the matter is nothing less than relatedness: the connection among writer, text, editor, reader, and the "nonliterary" public. This list comprises a large number of factions, all—once they are defined as factions—having urgent claims and concerns, often in conflict. But there is also a countertruth: that the boundaries separating these groups are in some sense, to some degree, unreal.

What writer is not a reader? What reader is not a writer? What editor is not both of these? "The two of us" who screened manuscripts in the office of *New England Review* were readers in every possible sense of the word. We were the audience of everyone who sent us work. In many cases, we may have been the *only* audience a given story or poem or essay ever had. And where is the writer, the editor, who does not come out of, and therefore belong to, that massive, mythically undignified, reputedly mindless thing we call the "general public"? And where is the citizen, however unliterary, who has not benefited, however unconsciously, from the lonely labor of the writer?

It's Us against Them, we sometimes think. But who are we? Who are they? What is the difference between us?

The history of poetry is haunted by the idea of audience in exactly the same way the history of romance is haunted by the idea of the Beloved and the history of war by the idea of the Evil Empire. Philosophy, psychology, and critical theory (in that order) have labored for at least three hundred years to express how Otherness is a creation of desire, of our need to explain ourselves to ourselves even while we are doing things we only half understand. And yet we go on, as we will go on as long as we last: all of us lovers, all of us soldiers, all of us poets, imagining we are called into action by something out there that needs us to love it or to kill it or to speak toward it some utterance that resonates with the mystery of being.

For poets, the image of audience is a double-edged cliché, as old as the art, but still dangerous whatever way it is posed. "For whom does the poet write?" is an expression of the left wing of the issue and "Who cares what the poet writes?" an expression of the right. The usual answers are equally polarized. To the first, the boundaries of reply are "for everyone" or "for myself alone"; to the second, "nobody" or "anybody." Politics enters as soon as the question is in the air. Populist, elitist, solipsistic: the gradations of possibility are as numerous as the history of argument is long. It is useful for poets to give an account of what is in their minds—vis-à-vis audience, vis-à-vis anything—when they are writing, to help us understand the particularities of motivation and the inner workings of craft; but I want to reserve space for what I believe is a healthy agnosticism about what they (and what I) have to say on the subject, hypothesizing that this issue more than most calls forth our natural perversity. What do we think about the Beloved while we are busy conceiving children? What do we think about the Great Satan of the enemy while we are busy waging war (or about the very same Evil Incarnate when, five years on, he or she has become our ally)? It matters to us at the time: but how much difference does it make to our children or to the battlefield dead? Ghosts are ghosts regardless, whether they are images of those who have come and gone before us or of those who will come and go after we ourselves have come and gone. We can only guess at who they were or will be based on what we know of ourselves.

All this is true also of the potential reader. And while it most certainly makes a difference how a given writer conceives that reader—just as it makes a difference what our political convictions are—it is also true that the conceived reader is a fabrication based on convenience, a preliminary creation that helps us to write the sort of poem we most want to write. The poem I write for the Beloved will certainly be different from the poem I write for my mother, or a critic, or Everyman. Do I decide to write for only one of these possibilities? If so, how do I make that decision, and what does it mean that I make it? In what guise do I decide? Into what or whom does my decision turn me? The history of romance is haunted as much by the image of the Lover as by that of the Beloved, and the history of war as much by the image of the Chosen People as by that of the Evil Empire. The proposition is always precisely double; the mirror can't help looking two ways.

I'm tempted simply to say that the best exploration of this problem I've ever encountered is Walter Ong's justly famous essay "The Writer's Audience Is Always a Fiction," to refer the reader there, and to wash my hands of the whole difficult business. Ong gives lucid expression to what is, for me, a clear and realistic hope:

> If the writer succeeds in writing, it is generally because he can
> fictionalize in his imagination an audience he has learned to know
> not from daily life but from earlier writers who were fictionalizing
> in their imagination audiences they had learned to know in still
> earlier writers, and so on back to the dawn of written narrative. If
> and when he becomes truly adept, an "original writer," he can do
> more than project the earlier audience, *he can alter it* (italics added).

But the romance haunts me, too, and I know that if I could give an honest and complete answer to the question "For whom do I write?" I would understand something important about the perverse dwarf who labors away in the sweatshop of my upper brain, making things I call poems. I believe I am entitled to say this much: that every poem is written exactly for whoever happens to be reading it at any given moment, and that if no one is reading it, for all practical purposes it does not exist. That person—the *actual* reader—is in one important way like the issue of the Lover and the Beloved: my ideas about the future determine nothing about the color of my child's hair, the shape of her hands, the quickness of her nerves; my ideas about my audience cannot determine the actuality of whatever audience I am fortunate enough to have, a second from now or in a hundred years. But this is not a sheerly fatalistic proposition. Children, poems, readers are not created *ex nihilo*; they are called forth in their different ways from the stuff we are given by the world—flesh, society, language, and the material history of process, which we both understand and misunderstand, use and misuse, in the course of our impossible passion to live forever and know everything.

In what I have said so far, it may sound as if my stance is essentially existential, that my belief is that we are all separate from each other, sealed off in hermetic subjectivities and busily projecting exterior realities in order to maintain an illusion of sanity, but that is not my position. We are constantly in danger of falling into such an atomized condition; but one antidote among others is the sort of body politic, tenuous though it may be, created by the bond between writer and reader through the medium of text. Reading is relationship, and so is writing; language is as communal, and as specifically human, as our flesh and blood, which we are born to share. But language is even more ours than flesh and blood are; insofar as we can be said to be creators at all, language is our creation.

Generally, we believe that our children are what they are because we have been attracted to some Other—something in the genes calls to something in the genes; we choose, we do not choose; we are chosen. In the best of circumstances, we do have at least something to say about it; in the worst (in the case of rape, say, as advocates of freedom of choice concerning abortion argue, or in the case of passionate error) we make our choices ex post facto. One of the beauties of the act of art is that we have more choices: to write or not to write, to read or not to read. We read with most profound pleasure and benefit those texts that at least appear to have been written with us in mind; we tend to reject those that seem too foreign. But what can it mean if I find that Dickinson or Yeats or Keats or Sappho *has me in mind?* Which me? And in what mind?

My impulse is to look for paradigms in other realms to understand how writer and reader create each other in the act of attention that we call poetry. I have understood more and more clearly with the passing of time how much my turning to poetry depended on the place where I grew up and the time when I grew up there. I was born in Noxubee County, Mississippi, in 1950, white and solidly rural working class in a part of the world where 70 percent of the population was black, deeply poor, and powerless in every sense. I lived there, as James Agee puts it, "successfully disguised to myself as a child." I grew up also a perfect little racist in that remote and otherwise benighted place, having from the very beginning no choice in the matter.

We have come to understand something about what racism inflicts on those who are its targets: racism on that level is violence, even when no shots are fired and no blood is shed. What is harder to understand, much less care about, is what racism does to racists, and to their children, whose beautiful childhood disguises come to include white robes and hoods.

Racism is a sort of bewitchment, made beautiful by the power of its awful magic to those it possesses, and language is part of the spell. That's why I don't entirely trust language and its figures, though I love them. To break the spell that was cast on me I had to die and come back as somebody else; I had to commit a long, slow suicide. That was the only available cure. Fortunately, I did not have to do this alone. I owe a debt for my unbewitching first and foremost to the heroes of the civil rights movement—an endeavor as important to whites and others as to blacks. Without that large and visible movement, and the obvious human logic upon which it was based, I would never have understood that I was not who I thought I was—one of the favored of the gods, one of the chosen—but was, in this metaphorical sense, one who deserved the suicide I granted myself.

I can now see that I first came to the writing of poetry, in 1970 or so, at the end of a process of self-dismantlement; and I came to it for what at first glance would appear to be all the wrong reasons: not in love and joy, but in exhaustion and horror and self-loathing. I would like to be able to say that, having worked my way carefully through the sort of self-analysis that clarifies the boundary between personal psychology and politics, I arrived fully at an empowered selfhood, ready to take on large and responsible social tasks, and that I found in poetry a perfect means to that end. In fact, nothing could be further from the truth. Instead, the process I went through was more emotional and intuitive than analytical—confused as it was with the more usual process of coming to terms with identity normal in adolescence—and when I came out the other end of it, there was little left of me but anger and guilt. I felt that something monstrous had been done to me, as indeed it had; but I was not ready to accept my own complicity in that process, much less my responsibility in taking part in the obvious struggles. Though this was not consciously in my mind at the time, I am afraid I turned to poetry as an escape. "What," some part of me must have thought, "could be further from what I came from than poetry? What could be more truly apolitical than this?" Where I grew up, people did not hate poetry; far from it. We did not think about poetry at all. Southerners are fond of talking about the great tradition of writing in the region; my earliest memory of discussion of a "great" writer is hearing someone curse "Faulkner, that traitor to the South." Poets got less than short shrift; they got no shrift at all. What, then, could be better? In the depths of my self-alienation, I think I believed poetry could belong to me alone. It was a narcissistic obsession, a passion without risk to its perpetrator because it was insulated from effects, like that of the Peeping Tom who believes the person he stares at anonymously through a window is passionately in love with him.

What I could not have known was that this obsession held within itself the seeds of its own healing. What I now understand is that poetry is stubbornly, radically communal, like all art. It belongs to no one, it is in love with no one, it serves no one: it simply relates. It is one of our great structures of relationship—by no means the only one, and no better (but no worse) than others—and thus the "birth" of a poet *as* poet is a birth into relatedness. No child comes into the world without parents, however broken the family may be. When I came to consciousness as a poet and found myself alone, I was already misunderstanding myself. Poetry can never truly serve narcissism because by its very being it implies progenitors and demands an audience. An utterly narcissistic writer—one who *truly* writes out of and for himself or herself alone—is an impossibility, a contradiction in terms.

I offer, therefore, a different paradigm, one that is perhaps the basis of my conception of audience.

My great-grandfather Tom Jackson died in 1957 at the age of ninety-seven; he was born in 1860, the year before the outbreak of the Civil War, and he died when I was seven because he fell down the stairs of his old farmhouse, broke his hip, and had to go to the hospital, where doctors accomplished in a week what just under a century of genuinely hard life had failed to do. His death was the first that came close to me; his funeral was the first I ever attended. Curiously, I remember standing in our living room on the day before he died, staring up at a row of books (a set of *Readers' Digest Condensed Books*) and thinking "Grandaddy is going to die"; then, when he did die, I felt a certain exaltation, as if I were a prophet for predicting the obvious and mentioning it only to myself.

But as far as I was concerned, Tom Jackson was no common man, and his dying deserved prophesying. He was the oldest white man anybody in our part of the country knew; and because he was white, the dating of his birth was precise, unlike that of an antebellum black person, who would have been by definition a slave. His age, like everything that belonged to white people, was authoritative.

I visited him fairly regularly throughout my early childhood; his presence is among my earliest memories. As I recall them, the visits were always the same. I never went to see him alone, partly because I was too young and partly because, well, one of my generation simply *wouldn't* go to his house alone; it would have been a breach of decorum. As I remember, it was always either my father or my grandmother (Tom Jackson's daughter) who took me there. We would invariably find him in one of two places: in his living room by the butane space heater when the weather was cold or on the front porch in his rocker when it was fine. Because his blood pressure was low, he was constantly chilled, and seemed always to be wearing more clothes than any normal human being would want to wear— even in Mississippi in August he would have on long underwear and a long-sleeved khaki workshirt; in winter, his butane heater was like the Old Testament furnace. He carried about him his own atmosphere: perfect for him, uncomfortable for others.

He was a splendidly archetypal old man in appearance—properly wrinkled and liver-spotted, with plenty of snow-white hair. He had the bleary bluish eyes of one who has survived the ordeal of old-fashioned cataract surgery (the sort where the convalescent must lie for months without moving his head, on threat of blindness or worse). He was most certainly a survivor. He could remember the Civil War and Reconstruction (he was the "man of the farm" at nine and claimed he could plow a straight row with a mule at that age, an astonishing accomplishment if true) and all the wars and reversals that succeeded. Wars and reversals were all he knew, but those he knew intimately. His presence was formidable; he was clear-minded, intelligent (though uneducated), forceful, arrogant, sure of himself and of his position in the family. He was a classical patriarch, and it is no wonder that my early images of God the Father, about whom I heard so much at the little Methodist church we attended, were all mixed up with Tom Jackson.

A child approaching him had to be announced. Tom Jackson made no pretense of remembering his great-grandchildren as individuals. He had thirteen children, a host of grandchildren, and a multitude of ones like me; our lives to him were frail, like the dandelions in his front yard, like spit on a hot stove. He'd see us coming, a large one and a small one; he'd rivet his gaze on the small one first, and say, "Whose child are you?" The hierophant adult then was required to answer, in my case, "This is Vernon's boy, Grandaddy," at which he then would say, "Well, let him come over here and shake my hand."

The handshake: this was a critical juncture. Tom Jackson had never owned much, but almost everything he'd ever owned he still had. This was true of cars and trucks, wagons and tractors; it was true of animals; it was true of the furniture in the house, the books in his bookshelves (few and strange—Masonic manuals and anti-Catholic tracts, with a healthy leavening of old *National Geographics* that belonged actually to my great-uncle Warren), his tenant farmers, and the parts of his body. He had all his hair, all his teeth, his tonsils, his appendix, everything he was born with, a catalog he would recite with pride. The one glaring exception was his good right hand, which he'd lost eons earlier in a run-in with a corn auger, maybe the only argument he couldn't win by sheer force of will. His hand was gone just at the wrist, and the resulting stump had been wrought into a sort of blunt point that always peeked suggestively out of the cuff of his khaki shirt. To a five- or six-year-old, this vision—this wound, this scar, this loss, this astonishing difference—was a source of horrified fascination. To shake hands with Grandaddy meant first the transgression of shaking left-handed—do children, boys, still receive careful instruction from their fathers in the art of shaking hands, "With the right, son, always with the right"?—and second the fraught opportunity of glimpsing what one ought to have been grasping but would never grasp. Perhaps there was something phallic about it—a notion that might have pleased the old man if it had ever secretly crossed his mind; but I am certain it never did, because he was as cruelly pure as a Baptist preacher, and as resolutely ignorant as he was smart. But to grasp his left hand was to transmigrate into his atmosphere, to enter the looking glass.

"When you begin to read a poem," Randall Jarrell writes in "The Obscurity of the Poet,"

> you are entering a foreign country whose laws and language and life are a kind of translation of your own; but to accept it because its stews taste exactly like your old mother's hash, or to reject it because the owl-headed goddess of wisdom in its temple is fatter than the Statue of Liberty, is an equal mark of that want of imagination, that inaccessibility to experience, of which each of us who dies a natural death will die.

Entering the foreign country of my great-grandfather's front porch, I was already learning something about the kind of experience poetry is. I was learning to cross boundaries with balanced fear and fascination, disgust and longing.

Finally, having done what was required of me, I would meet one of two fates: either I would be dismissed to play in the yard or in the front hall until the adults had finished their visit; or I would be told a story. How can I say which I dreaded more? Playing at Grandaddy's was boring. That was no country for children; there was nothing to play *with*, except the walking canes and rocking chairs of the old, Byzantium writ backwards. But to hear a story: that, too, was no pleasure to me, because Grandaddy was a terrifying storyteller, and yet the stories, I thought, were incomprehensible and dull. That shows how little I knew. It is certainly true that while he loved to tell stories, he was interested in only a few, telling the same ones again and again: the one I simply could not understand, for instance, about how his father died in a Yankee prison camp, and when the Federals came marching into Louisville, Mississippi, in 1865, Tom Jackson stood on top of a split-rail fence shouting, "You killed my father!" at the top of his lungs until he lost his balance and fell on his butt—and all the bluebellies laughed; or the one about how, after the war, the family had no salt and so had to dig up the smokehouse floor and eat the salty dirt. How could I understand these things at five or six? He made no effort to explain them to me. I had little idea of what the Civil War had been, or why the soldiers laughed at the pain of the boy (just my age!), or why anyone would *have* to eat dirt, salt or no salt.

But the truly terrifying thing was the guise he assumed as he spoke. This was no pleasant and loving storytelling in which my parents indulged me; rather, it was as if I was not even there. Tom Jackson would stare off into the distance with his otherworldly old man's eyes, and he would say what he had to say. His authority was clearly absolute in his own mind. It was an authority based on two things: a monstrous ego and an infinite memory. He was who he was, and he had seen what he had seen. This was neither entertainment nor instruction; this was testimony, something like prophesy in reverse. I was to understand that I was in the presence of a Personage, a redneck oracle, and it was not his job to explain nor mine to understand—he was there to speak what he remembered, and I was there to remember what he spoke.

It gives me no comfort to imagine Tom Jackson as a paradigm for anything in my life. He was, I understand by reading between the lines of our family history, a tyrant and a bully; he steamrollered his wife and broke the spirits of most of his children (my grandmother excepted; she inherited enough of his iron and invented sufficient grace of her own to stand eye to eye with him). He was an unrepentant and unreconstructed man who lived by will and bleak hard work, owned land, had many children, and expected no more and no less of those around him. He was the image of a antediluvian (but postlapsarian) patriarch, and patriarchs as we all know are in bad odor for good reason.

But there is a point—a bad and profound pun—that simply cannot be missed here: when I went to visit Tom Jackson, my visit was an *audience*. I was granted, in a large and ancient sense, a visitation and a hearing. His presence, in the act of his storytelling, was transpersonal—the audience I had with him was in fact with history, and the audience he had in me was in fact with the future. Not that either of us had any such thing in mind: it just worked out that way.

I would not want to imagine that the self I project in a poem is anything like Tom Jackson—his narration was too fascistic for me to wish to imitate it. Neither do I want to believe that the reader I project for myself through the poem is as helpless as the five-year-old boy excruciatingly transfixed on that Mississippi porch. In any case, the whole setup is so terribly, so archetypally southern—so like a scene from great-grandaddy Faulkner—that I don't like to look at it from any angle that is not oblique. Perhaps that's a failure in me; perhaps it isn't.

But I learned from Tom Jackson that an audience is double: that there is a level of utterance that is mutually and reflexively creative. Whatever else I inherit from him, I inherit the best and most transpersonal moments he shared with me—those moments when he did not give a good goddamn who I was—and with them the means to extend Ong's accurate observation by one human degree:

> If the writer succeeds in writing, it is generally because he can fictionalize in his imagination an audience he has learned to know not from daily life but from earlier writers who were fictionalizing in their imagination audiences they had learned to know in still earlier writers, and so on back to the dawn of written narrative. If and when he becomes truly adept, an "original writer," he can do more than project the earlier audience, he can alter it.

I take this to mean that while we are apprentices, we inherit our concept of audience *along with* the craft that we labor to learn, like taking the medicine with sugar. The Dear Reader to whom we imagine we are writing is a dead convention, exactly like meter and rhyme, or narrative structure, or image, or trope, or what have you. One learns a craft of audience along with the craft of language; and one's craft of audience will depend on whether one is learning from Larkin or Plath or Whitman or Rich. We are all readers before we are writers; we know how it feels to be written for by a Whitman or a Plath. Somehow they have us in mind, and we aspire to write poems of our own in order to reproduce that experience for others. It is at best a generous, humble, and communal impulse that is muddied by sheer ego, the desire to be such a powerful, prophetic mind that can have in itself the whole of the past and also of a future world of readers, containing even me, however reluctant I may be to join a club that would have me as a member.

But there comes a moment when a line is crossed, when the poet takes hold of something by the left hand—by which I mean nothing more mystical than that the poet as poet understands and respects the strangeness of his or her own life and of the lives of others, and grasps that strangeness by whatever means present themselves, realizing that there is no prophesy and no prophet, but only a desperate humanity staving off death by the things we tell each other—and then the poet alters the projected audience by withdrawing the projection. By this, I mean that the poet ceases to write for some conventionalized particular and begins to write a poem that belongs to no one, is in love with no one, serves no one. This does not mean that it is *written* for no one. It means that the poet consciously writes a poem that is for the actual reader—for whatever reader will read it at any given moment. And it is devoutly to be hoped that the reader will be equal to the demand of being created at that moment, along with the poem itself, which without the *actual* reader is less than nothing.

Laughed Off

Canon, *Kharakter,* and the Dismissal of Vachel Lindsay

The priest departs, the divine literatus comes.
—Walt Whitman

It must be tough to be a poet.
—Vachel Lindsay's milkman

Oh gawd!!!
—Ezra Pound

It is arguable whether, as Virginia Woolf famously wrote, "on or about December 1910 human character changed." It is also arguable exactly what she meant when she wrote it. If the usual interpretation—that Woolf is describing the birth of modernism—were correct, and if the resulting timetable were the literal truth, then the suicide of the American poet Vachel Lindsay on December 5, 1931, precisely twenty-one years after Woolf's transformative month, could be regarded as coinciding with the arrival of modernism's difficult adulthood.

Eleanor Ruggles, one of Lindsay's biographers, provides this account of his death:

> [Lindsay's wife Elizabeth] was awakened by a crash below. Then she heard other noises, then rapid but extraordinarily heavy footsteps thudding along the lower hall, and then Vachel crawling up the almost perpendicular stairs on his hands and knees with unbelievable swiftness and force. Her instant thought was that he had had some hideous seizure, had reverted completely to the subhuman, and was coming up to finish off her and the sleeping children. . . . But the moment she saw him running through the upstairs hall with his hands raised, she knew it was for him she should be afraid. His eyes were distended; his face was white, wild and terrified. . . . [H]e asked for water and when she brought it managed to say, in reply to her anguished questioning, "I tried to kill myself by drinking Lysol."
>
> As she was hurrying from the bedroom to call Dr. McMeen, he threw down the glass and shook his fists in the air and gasped out something to the effect that "I got them before they could get me—they can just try to explain this, if they can!" (431–32)

The poet Edgar Lee Masters, in his biography *Vachel Lindsay: A Poet in America*, adds the following details:

> When Mrs. Lindsay went downstairs she found her picture and those of the children propped around the table centerpiece with two lighted candles burning before them. In the bathroom she found a tea-glass stained with lysol, and a large empty bottle of lysol. On the floor was a pillow from the library, and a picture of Mrs. Lindsay at seventeen propped over the little blue coat of Susan, his little daughter.

In December 1910, on the other hand, Vachel Lindsay was thirty-one years old, living with his parents in Springfield, Illinois, personally and professionally at a loss—to all appearances, at any rate. "I loafed around Springfield as the town dolt," Lindsay wrote of the

period between 1908 and 1912 (Ruggles 144). *Poetry* magazine
founder Harriet Monroe, who doubtless had it straight from Lindsay himself, mentions "that winter of 1909–10, when the preacher-
strain in him almost conquered, and we find him an itinerant lecturer for the Anti-Saloon League—a winter illuminated by the dim
dawning of a consciousness that his own special art was poetry"
(*Poets and Their Art* 22); and for December of Woolf's *annus mirabi-
lis*, Ruggles records only that Lindsay gave a talk at the local YMCA,
a "Ruskin Revival" attended by a "scant" thirty people.

Arrogant, intelligent, willfully provincial, the young Lindsay was
a furious autodidact. Accounts of his life and especially his corre-
spondence reveal that Lindsay's most striking characteristic in adolescence and young manhood was his unwavering sense of mission.
Brought up a "middle westerner of the middle class," as Amy Lowell
called him with gentle disparagement (Chénetier xxiv), the son of
a doctor and a Disciples of Christ Sunday School teacher, Lindsay
early came to consider himself chosen: though to do precisely what
he was for a long time uncertain. He believed early on that he had a
gift for poetry as well as for the visual arts. His parents had a good
library, and his first profound experiences with books came early.

> At eight, he first read *Paradise Lost*, that most subtly passionate of
> poems, and fell permanently in love with Milton's own love, the
> goldenhaired beguiling Eve.
>
> He was thirteen when he asked his mother one evening, "Who
> was Edgar Allan Poe?" to which Mrs. Lindsay replied in her positive
> way: "He was a very talented young man who died drunk on the
> streets of Baltimore. He wrote poetry. I think we have his poetry
> here." . . . Vachel read [Poe] all through that night. The haunting
> "Ulalume" was his favorite of Poe's poems, perhaps of all poems,
> and the tragic gallant writer of it became his fascination. "Poe," he
> declares, "was always a kind of Egyptian to me." (Ruggles 41)

Lindsay's early reading stayed with him. In 1908 he wrote to Rich-
ard Watson Gilder, editor of the *Century Magazine*, that

> My first love among the Poets was Edgar Poe—when I first entered
> High School. I could have been called a Poe-crank for my whole
> High School period. Thinking it all over now, without the book of
> poems in my hand, in a most matter-of-fact mood—I can say that
> Ulalume is one of the great works of art to me, and no other work of
> his has the same staying power—I know of nothing in the catalogue
> of beautiful things for which I have more respect. (*Letters* 29)

He was also in love with Beardsley, with Blake (the artist at least as
much as the poet), and with the Pre-Raphaelites; he left Hiram College to pursue his mission in art, first at the Chicago Art Institute
(1901–3) and then at the New York School of Art, where he studied
painting and drawing with Robert Henri.

It was around this time that Lindsay began to create—*write*
would be too limited a word—his first "visionary" book of poems
and drawings, *Where Is Aladdin's Lamp?*, which he later destroyed.
He also printed illustrated broadsides of two or three of his poems
and attempted to peddle them in Times Square and on the New
York streets, with predictable results. He taught classes in art and
history and literature at the New York YMCA, at first for no pay, later
for a pittance; and—according to Marc Chénetier, editor of *Letters of
Vachel Lindsay*—"Throughout the year, VL has visions, particularly
on December 23" (xix).

Who would have predicted that by 1915 so thoroughly unpromis-
ing a "Poe-crank" as Nicholas Vachel Lindsay of Springfield, Illinois,
would be one of the most visible poets in the United States?

Who besides Lindsay himself?

It was in early 1914 that Lindsay first began to make a real reputation. Invited to read his new poem "The Congo" at Springfield's
Lincoln Day banquet on February 12—a date dangerously close to
Lindsay's beloved Valentine's Day—he nervously rehearsed the
poem for his friends, introducing "a nasal but musical chanting like
the Gregorian chant he used to hear at the Paulist fathers' church"
(Ruggles 215).

Fat black bucks in a wine-barrel room,
Barrel-house kings, with feet unstable,
Sagged and reeled and pounded on the table,
Pounded on the table,   *A deep rolling bass.*
Beat an empty barrel with the handle of a broom,
Boom, boom, boom,
With a silk umbrella and the handle of a broom.
Boomlay, boomlay, boomlay, boom.
Then I had religion, then I had a vision.
I could not turn from their revel in derision.   *More deliberate.*
Then I saw the Congo, creeping through the black, *Solemnly chanted.*
Cutting through the forest with a golden track.
Then along that riverbank
A thousand miles
Tattooed cannibals danced in files;
Then I heard the boom of the blood-lust song   *A rapidly piling*
And a thigh-bone beating on a tin-pan gong.   *climax of speed*
And "blood" screamed the whistles and the   *and racket.*
 fifes of the warriors. . . .
"Boomlay, boomlay, boomlay, boom,"   *With a philosophic*
A roaring, epic, rag-time tune   *pause.*
From the mouth of the Congo
To the Mountains of the Moon. . . .
"Be careful what you do,
Or Mumbo-Jumbo, God of the Congo,   *All the o sounds*
And all of the other   *very golden.*
Gods of the Congo,   *Heavy accents very*
                                                   heavy.
Mumbo-Jumbo will hoo-doo you,   *Light accents very*
                                                   light.
Mumbo-Jumbo will hoo-doo you,   *Last line*
Mumbo-Jumbo will hoo-doo you."   *whispered.*

One of his enduringly successful performance pieces, "The Congo,"
less than a third of which is excerpted here, demonstrates all aspects
of Lindsay's style at its height: the heavy dactylic rhythms, the pyro-

technic rhymes, the stagy repetitions, the choreographed effects—Rudy Vallee out of Billy Sunday, with an odd (and completely coincidental) grafting of Gerard Manley Hopkins.

Ruggles tells us that Lindsay came to write "The Congo" after hearing a sermon about the death of a missionary in Africa.

> Lindsay was sitting with his parents in their pew in the third row when suddenly all the panorama of the Negro race flashed into his mind. He remembered from his childhood the pious ecstasies of black Lucy, their cook. He remembered the waiters around the woodpile at the Leland rocked by laughter as by a force outside themselves. He remembered Charlie Gibbs, Springfield's gigantic Negro lawyer, who was surely born to prance on the riverbank with a coffin-headed shield and a shovel spear. . . . According to legend, Lindsay went home after church and dashed off "the Congo," his most famous poem, before Sunday dinner. Actually the writing took him about two months and he did more polishing than on any poem before. . . . His intention in writing "The Congo" was to portray the concern of a savage, childlike race with religion, a concern that will in the end redeem the soul of the race. (212, 214)

When he first performed the poem locally, neither the citizens of Springfield nor Lindsay's family were quite prepared to see him "throw back his head and . . . emit his barbaric 'Boomlays' ('Simply bellowing,' remarked one of them)," or to watch

> his eyes begin to roll like a man's in a fit and his hands shoot from the cuffs of his dress suit and jab the air and his body rock and shoulders weave. . . . The performance took seven minutes. As it went on and on, a few people turned away their heads to hide their embarrassment but many more let out snorts and giggles that swelled a rising wave of laughter. (215)

A month later, when he performed the poem again—this time in Chicago at a banquet sponsored by Harriet Monroe and *Poetry* magazine, with Carl Sandburg, Arthur Ficke, and no less a person-

age than William Butler Yeats in the room—the reception was rather
different.

> It was the end of an overlong program. The weary listeners had had
> enough and some were on their feet ready to go home. But Lindsay's
> beginning lines, droned and pulselike, arrested them: ". . . Boom,
> boom, boom!" "That 'boom,'" says an ear-witness, "shook the room.
> . . ." The audience burst into applause. The Negro waiters against
> the walls applauded. The guest of honor, jerked from the misty
> kingdom of his Celtic imaginings, must have felt like one who pats
> a kitten and sees it turn into a lion, and there were bravos from
> Lindsay's fellow midwesterners, persuading him into reciting "General
> Booth." (217–18)

Clearly impressed, Yeats inquired of him, "What are we going to do
to restore the primitive singing of poetry?" (Engler 29).

This was a far cry from the reception Lindsay had received in his
hometown, where, as Paul Gray describes it, he sounded "queer"
because "his experimentations had led him back to the oldest style
of poetic recitation, the chant," but in a new American form, replete
with "whoops, yells, booms, cheers—all the exuberant noises and
rhythms he found in American life" (220). The difference in response
to "The Congo" between February and March may well have
felt to Lindsay like a change in human character; in any case, from
this moment he was—as much as any poet ever is—made.

This difference cannot be satisfactorily explained simply by the
fact that in Chicago he was reciting not to the Springfield gentility,
but to a tired, bored literary group. Poets by no means agreed about
Lindsay. T. S. Eliot, for instance, could never abide his poems. "I was
appalled by Lindsay," he says in a 1920 letter to John Gould Fletcher
(Letters v. 1, 410); elsewhere, having attended a Lindsay performance,
he dismisses Lindsay as "impossible" (Chénetier 210). As for
Pound, Humphrey Carpenter tells us that "when he eventually observed
Lindsay he simply said, 'Oh gawd!!!'" Never admired by any
of the torchbearers of high modernism, Lindsay billed himself as a

poet of the people. His admirers "could total half a million or a million—if all my audiences were added up these ten years," he would write in a letter in 1923. "And they—my audiences—always evoke the same mood . . . always my audience *loves* me. . . . I can win an audience in five minutes" (*Letters* 297–98). But his debut reversed that polarity—it was the literary establishment that rescued him from the obscurity of Springfield and launched a career that would shortly become a national phenomenon.

Vachel Lindsay was and is a problem—man, poet, figure, he is problematic in every possible sense. The rise of his public career was precipitous; so was its decline. In the "Chronology" at the beginning of his selection of Lindsay's letters, Marc Chénetier records for 1911 that "VL becomes a construction worker for two months," for 1915 that "Lindsay recites for President Wilson's cabinet in February," and for 1918–19 "VL recites all over the United States" (xx–xxi). It is clear enough that by 1920, the mission to which Lindsay felt called was not merely a self-fabrication; it was the shared projection of a significant audience. Writing in 1924, Harriet Monroe says of him that "the obscure aspirant of ten years ago has become probably the best and farthest known of all our American poets of this vocal decade" (*Poets and Their Art* 21).*

---

*I retain this information as Chénetier cites it, although Catherine Wakefield Ward, niece of Vachel Lindsay, notes that it is probably "inflated from what NVL himself reported of his triumphant dinner party in Washington, D.C., at the Vroomans' house" (pers. comm., August 14, 1992). She calls my attention to Lindsay's own published account, in his autobiographical introduction to *The Collected Poems of Vachel Lindsay*, where he describes "one of the thrilling memories of my life when I was entetained in Washington by the Honorable and Mrs. Carl Vrooman. Carl Vrooman was then Assistant Secretary of Agriculture. The song I sang that seemed to mean the most in Washington was that of 'The Rose and the Lotus.' Franklin K. Lane, the then Secretary of the Interior, did me the honor to print it and send it to both Houses of Congress and to all those interested in a special way in the opening of the Panama Canal and the opening of the Panama-Pacific exposition at San Francisco. *It is the nearest that my life has come to politics*" (xiii, italics added).

It is equally clear that by the end of Lindsay's life, something had seriously altered that mission, the man who embodied it, the audience that desired it, or all three. It will not do to say—as Ruggles very rightly points out—that Lindsay committed suicide because of a spoiled career: "It was not his debts—whose extent, said Elizabeth, he grasped only vaguely—nor was it the public neglect of his work, nor even the dimming of his muse that wholly undid him at the last. He was ill" (429). It will not do to make Lindsay's suicide a Romantic emblem.

The course of his career is no easier to comprehend. His demise as a poet is no more, and no less, problematic than the fact that he rose in the first place. What made Vachel Lindsay, the poet? What unmade him? How could it all have happened so vertiginously? Why did it happen when it did, to him and not to somebody else? And what does the fate of Vachel Lindsay have to do with that literary ferment of the early decades of the twentieth century to which we give the name *modernism*?

It is not possible to answer these questions with certainty or finality—not in a single essay, not in the whole course of literary history. That is precisely why they are not only interesting but also vital. Seen in a certain light, Vachel Lindsay's image is a microcosm of literary reception and lack thereof; in him, the lines of tension linking fame and oblivion, revolution and convention, artifact and personality, text and performance—poet, poem, critic, reader, listener, culture—cross and recross themselves until they tangle in an inextricable knot. The mystery of Vachel Lindsay is a subset of the mystery of canon: What writers enter, and what texts? What audiences have access to them and influence over them? Who or what decides?

Late-twentieth-century critical response to Lindsay is relatively rare; when critics discuss him, they usually make him an object of derision or an emblem (usually from a conservative perspective) of marginalization. Writing from the literary center, in a September

1991 issue of the *New York Review of Books*, Elizabeth Hardwick reports,

> It was in California that Lindsay learned of the death of General William Booth, founder of the Salvation Army. And thus he came to write one of his first bizarre incantations ["General William Booth Enters Into Heaven"], an unaccountable success for which the mind glancing back on our literary history is, well, *dumbstruck*. (10)

Though she concedes, "There is always a market for 'carrying on' in public" (11), Hardwick is astonished that anybody, anywhere, ever took Lindsay seriously. "As a versifier," she tells us, "he had no more caution than a hobo hitching a ride, but somehow his voice prevailed for a time, even with some of the respected critics of the day" (9)—implicitly suggesting that Lindsay's ephemeral prominence can be accounted for only by a failure of the tastemakers.

And yet his "carrying on" filled huge auditoriums. Upstate New York novelist and essayist Carl Carmer, who was a student at Harvard when he heard Lindsay perform, declared, "Tennyson was a pale wraith within us as Lindsay's bold accents beat the living daylights out of our polite concepts of poetry!" Likewise, Carmer's contemporary John Dos Passos, who probably attended the same Harvard reading, wrote, "We went to kid, but were very much impressed in spite of ourselves" (Ruggles 237).

Writing from the literary left, in his 1989 book *Repression and Recovery: Modern American Poetry and the Politics of Cultural Memory, 1910–1945*, Cary Nelson warns,

> we need to stop thinking of artistic failure as a statement only about individual tragedy or the weaknesses and limitations of individual character and begin to see it as culturally driven, as a complex reflection of social and historical contradictions, as the result of the risks of decisions made in a network of determinations. In that context Vachel Lindsay's doomed fantasy of a truly public and participatory democratic poetry becomes, say, as important to our sense

of culture as T. S. Eliot's virtually decisive co-optation of modernism in *The Waste Land*.

In Lindsay's case, it is partly his failure to achieve his impossible ambitions—ambitions extracted from ideals circulating in the culture at large—that is his gift to future generations. (69)

Nelson is no more ready than Hardwick to defend the staying power of Lindsay's poems themselves; in any case, Lindsay is scarcely more than an aside in Nelson's valuable study of American poets from the early twentieth century—Mike Quin, Arturo Giovannitti, Anna Louise Strong, Stanley Kimmel, Mike Gold, H. H. Lewis (the "Plowboy Poet" of Missouri), Walter Conrad Arensberg, Genevieve Taggard, Edwin Rolfe, Sol Funaroff, and many others—who were perpetual outsiders, achieving far less success at any point in their careers than Lindsay at his height.

Hardwick's response to Lindsay, though brilliantly and acerbically dismissive, is vague at crucial points. "General William Booth Enters into Heaven," one of Lindsay's three or four "famous" poems and one of his most popular performance pieces, she is forced to acknowledge "an unaccountable success"; and with the unexamined qualifier "somehow," she tells us that "his voice prevailed for a time." It is just at these points, no doubt, that Nelson would wish, quite rightly, to intervene and fill in the gaps with an account of the "culturally driven"; but Hardwick has implicitly anticipated him. Writing of the Edgar Lee Masters biography of Lindsay, Hardwick tells us,

> In the end, as [Masters] reaches Lindsay's declining audience and death, he begins to see the life as a social rather than a personal tragedy, to view the native "singer" as a victim of the East, the money-grubbing, alienated world that preferred the poems of [not, as one might expect, Eliot and Pound and Stevens and Moore, but] Robert Frost and E. A. Robinson, poets Masters finds essentially "English" in tone and landscape rather than American.

Then Hardwick quotes the following passage from Masters's biography:

The motley stocks and alien breeds which have taken America
cannot be American until there is an America to mold them into
Americans. . . . Did the East, did these alien stocks want to be
American? This is what Lindsay was up against. In this connection
mention must be made of the Jews. (9)

There are, one might conclude, cultural drives and cultural drives. A
reader can be "dumbstruck" by a poem, in more than one sense—
and likewise by a prejudice.

What is of crucial interest here is dismissiveness: just what does
it take to dismiss a poet? No poet of genuine visibility has ever been
more summarily dismissed—from the canon, from the classroom,
from the consciousness of readers—than Vachel Lindsay. And for
what? If idiosyncrasy, arrogance, and anti-Semitism are the crite-
ria—and in fact the anti-Semitism in the passage quoted above belongs to Masters, not Lindsay—then why should Ezra Pound not
join Lindsay in the outer darkness of the shadow of the modern?

At this point, it is tempting to say of Pound, as Auden did of
Paul Claudel, that we "pardon him for writing well." If we are in
fact willing to say this of Pound but not of Lindsay, then it might
be well to try to determine what we mean—as well as what Pound
meant, and what Lindsay meant, and what the world meant in
1910—by "writing well." If in 1938 Harriet Monroe can contend that
in his prime Lindsay wrote "immortal poems" (*A Poet's Life* 281) and
in 1990 Elizabeth Hardwick can find him an "extraordinary embarrassment" (10), we are faced with a clear lack of consensus. Given
Lindsay's fate as a poet and as a man, this difference has to be regarded, as Nelson warns, as more than a mere difference of personal
opinion, or as the symptom of a "merely" personal failure of character. On the other hand, character itself may be more than a "merely"
personal matter.

Like so many of his predecessors and his contemporaries, Vachel
Lindsay was out to forge a new poetry—and by extension, in his own
terms, a new soul—for America. American poetry and the character

of the American nation were for him, as for anyone of his Romantic/religious turn of mind, identical. Readers' responses to such a writer will inevitably be conditioned by their own metaphysical and political attitudes. Lindsay's religion-inflected patriotism is especially odious to Elizabeth Hardwick, who calls him

> a naïve, manic evangelist, preaching the Gospel of Beauty [Lindsay's own term for his religion of the aesthetic], and carrying with him on his incredible cross-country hikes the Christian fundamentalism and Anti-Saloon teachings of his youth. Along with, of course, Illinois, the prairie, the conviction of being the voice of some real America, *in situ*, that must be honored, as if under threat of extinction by a flood. (9)

And it is true that where Lindsay is most American is precisely where he is most problematic.

"National literatures," Toni Morrison recently observed,

> like writers, get along the best way they can, and with what they can. Yet they do seem to end up describing and inscribing what is really on the national mind. For the most part, the literature of the United States has taken as its concern the architecture of a *new white man*. (14–15)

Nowhere is this more apparent than in such a poem as "The Congo," where Lindsay is simultaneously forceful and—however unconsciously, however naïvely—paternalistic and racist.

Of course, the backhanded racism of "The Congo" is consonant with the time—it was on the national mind. A 1914 review in The New Republic praised the "savage imagery of [Lindsay's] lines, the riotous picture of the negro mind set against the weird background of the primitive Congo" ("Sincerity in the Making" 26). Ruggles herself, writing in the 1950s, is not critical of these attitudes; and Amy Lowell praised "The Congo," declaring "how often I pass a day with them, / Boomlaying and shouting, 'creeping through the black,' /

With a whole troop of nigger-gods yelling at my back" (*Critical Fable* 43). Certainly Lindsay did not think of himself as a racist. When "driven to think seriously about his Negro fellow citizens" by a race riot in Springfield in 1908, Lindsay—for whom Lincoln was manifestly a hero—declared in a speech that "The first requisition is to have a big heart for alien men," and years later told a friend that

> the only way to end lynching would be to thrust yourself into the thick of such a mob and make the men slay you instead of the Negro. "When they realized what they had done, their hearts would be touched, their consciences shocked." (Ruggles 138–39)

Another persistent story about Lindsay is equally instructive: the legend that he "discovered" Langston Hughes in 1925. Ruggles tells the story this way:

> In Washington, in the dining room of the Wardman Park Hotel, a brown-skinned bus boy in a white jacket ignored the senators and oil magnates, sidled shyly up to the wall table at which the only poet in the crowded room sat opposite his wife and laid a slim manuscript by Lindsay's plate. That evening Lindsay opened his recital in the little theater of the hotel by reading the poems the boy had given him. It was the beginning of fame for the young Negro poet Langston Hughes. (352)

To this account, which Ruggles takes at face value, Arnold Rampersad, Hughes's own biographer, adds important details. It is true that Hughes was working, temporarily, as a busboy at the Wardman Park Hotel—though he had recently worked as a reporter for the *Washington Sentinel* and as a research assistant to Carter G. Woodson, "one of the founders in 1916 of the Association for the Study of Negro Life and History, and editor of its influential *Journal of Negro History*" (100). According to Rampersad's ironic account, far from sidling "shyly" up to Lindsay's table, Hughes—who had already "tried to snare Carl Sandburg" on an earlier occasion—"pounced":

[D]ropping the poems on the table, he mumbled something about admiring Lindsay, then fled to the kitchen. Peering out from behind the pantry door he saw Lindsay finish his dinner, then leave the room.

That evening, Lindsay startled his large audience by announcing that he had discovered a poet, a bona fide poet, a *Negro* poet no less, working as a busboy in their very midst. As proof, he read all three poems to the audience. The next morning Hughes found several white reporters waiting to pepper him with questions about his poetic gift (curious in a Negro) and how he had come by it. Milking the moment, he answered all the questions with his practiced humility. . . . As for Lindsay, Hughes hoped to meet him, but had to leave on November 30 for New York, where he [Hughes] had appointments. (117)

The fact is that Hughes was already known, awarded, and published as a poet—he had won first prize, over Countee Cullen, in *Opportunity* magazine's poetry competition, and his first book, *The Weary Blues*, was on the brink of coming out (107, 116). Rampersad describes how

Lindsay, who had since discovered that his "discovery" had already published widely, with a book from Knopf, gamely met with Hughes for a few minutes. (119)

Evidently this is the only time Lindsay and Hughes ever met as man to man rather than as diner to busboy; Lindsay's opportunity to be a prophetic talent scout like Amy Lowell and Ezra Pound had fizzled. In a kind but unconsciously ironic gesture, Lindsay "left a gift for Hughes at the hotel office—a handsome two-volume set of Amy Lowell's biography of Keats" with a mini-essay on "The New Poetry" inscribed across "the first six leaves" (119). Lindsay's advice to Hughes is preserved in his *Letters*:

The "New Poetry" movement has been going on in America since 1912. Two members of that army have died—Joyce Kilmer in the war, and Amy Lowell very recently. Already one hundred distin-

guished books of verse or criticism have been written, and hundreds
of poems set going.

Eleven of the distinguished books are by Amy Lowell—and are
listed in the front of this one. Please read the books and ignore the
newspapers. I should say [Lowell's] *Tendencies in Modern American
Poetry* is a good book to start on. You may know all this better than I
do. (364)

Through all this, Lindsay's intentions are surely good; it is his
assumptions that are at fault. What more wonderful thing than to
discover a "primitive" black poet working as a busboy in the very
hotel where Lindsay is giving a reading? But it was not only Lindsay
who was taken in—so were the "white reporters" and the newspapers, which Lindsay of all people cautions Hughes to "ignore." And
Hughes, himself by necessity a fairly formidable self-promoter, rose
to the occasion: he returned from New York "at once to squeezing
what further publicity he could from the Vachel Lindsay episode.
Contacting Underwood and Underwood, the photographic news
agency, he hoisted a tray of dishes onto his shoulder for their cam-
eraman" (119).

"The Congo" is surely well intentioned, meant as a compliment
to what Lindsay, and America, would have perceived as the "primitive" energy of African culture. Still, it is poetry in blackface. At the
heart of the Higher Vaudeville one can discern the Romantic min-
strel as a literary clone of Mr. Bones, whose true function Toni Morrison, among others, has by now accurately discerned:

> In minstrelsy, a layer of blackness applied to a white face released
> it from law. Just as entertainers, through or by association with
> blackface, could render permissible topics that otherwise would
> have been taboo, so American writers were able to employ an imag-
> ined Africanist persona to articulate and imaginatively act out the
> forbidden in American culture. (66)

If this is true, then "The Congo" obviously must be read not as
about Africa but as a projection of America—just as a dream says

everything about the dreamer, and nothing about the subject of the dream. If Lindsay's projections of Africans and African Americans—and elsewhere of Asians, and of women—remain cartoons, this fact speaks to the limitation of his underlying psychospiritual theory about the nature of poetry *and* of America. All this could be written off, as Elizabeth Hardwick writes it off, as provincialism, the "innocence" of a local and limited point of view, symptomatic of Lindsay's allegiance to what he called the "New Localism," linked to his "Gospel of Beauty." But it may also be an effect of the arrogance of the American sovereign self, and Lindsay's unquestioning championing thereof. At root, Lindsay's impetus is religious, however much it pretends here and there to be purely aesthetic, merely a show. And his religion is of course the typically American, Emersonian religion of the divine self and its sacred Imagination, whose visions—when they present themselves as its purest products and not as overtly appropriative political gestures—must be, ipso facto, powerful, authoritative, true.

"[O]n or about December 1910 human character changed": Virginia Woolf's pronouncement comes from her essay "Mr. Bennett and Mrs. Brown," wherein she argues against the Edwardian novelist Arnold Bennett's charge that the novelists of Woolf's generation "are unable to create characters that are real, true, and convincing." Woolf continues,

> I am not saying that one went out, as one might into a garden, and there saw that a rose had flowered, or that a hen had laid an egg. The change was not sudden and definite like that. But a change there was, nevertheless; and, since one must be arbitrary, let us date it about the year 1910. . . . All human relations have shifted—those between masters and servants, husbands and wives, parents and children. And when human relations change there is at the same time a change in religion, conduct, politics, and literature. Let us agree to place one of these changes about the year 1910. (4–5)

Woolf does not attempt to define "human character." She finesses the pitfalls of such an impossible task by assuming that her audience knows what she means by the phrase, and by simultaneously, and significantly, blurring the distinction between the character of actual human beings and the construction of characters in novels. Her approach is graceful and subtle, but it does leave a certain amount of room for misunderstanding—and also for misquotation. Monroe Spears, in *Dionysus and the City: Modernism in Twentieth-Century Poetry*, renders Woolf thus:

> According to Virginia Woolf's famous statement, "on or about December, 1910, *human nature* changed"; as we have seen, the concept of biological mutation becomes prominent with the turn of the century; and the assumption that fundamental change in human nature is possible is essential to Marxist, anarchist, and other revolutionary political doctrines. (29; emphasis added)

A central tenet of Spears's argument is that modernism is founded on fundamental discontinuity, ruptures in the fabric of thought, history, the world—*metaphysical discontinuity, aesthetic discontinuity, rhetorical discontinuity,* and *temporal discontinuity* are the specific terms he uses. A change in human nature arriving as precipitously as a biological mutation would most certainly produce discontinuity in the human world. However, a change in human *character* would appear to be a rather different thing. Though Spears's misquote appears to be (pun intended) natural enough, the alteration makes a profound difference in Woolf's argument. Spears makes Woolf more a "modernist"—at least in his direly philosophical sense of the word—than she appears in fact to be.

In "Mr. Bennett and Mrs. Brown," Woolf is certainly interested in discontinuity; however, she is more concerned with discontinuity of style—in life as in novels—than with any fundamental shift in human nature, any harrowing rupture with history.

> In life one can see the change, if I may use a homely illustration, in the character of one's cook. The Victorian cook lived like a leviathan

in the lower depths, formidable, silent, obscure, inscrutable; the
Georgian cook is a creature of sunshine and fresh air, in and out of
the drawing-room, now to borrow *The Daily Herald*, now to ask for
a hat. Do you ask for more solemn instances of the power of the
human race to change? Read the *Agamemnon*, and see whether,
in process of time, your sympathies are not almost entirely with
Clytemnestra. Or consider the married life of the Carlyles, and
bewail the waste, the futility, for him and for her, of the horrible
domestic tradition which made it seemly for a woman of genius
to spend her time chasing beetles, scouring saucepans, instead of
writing books. (5)

Woolf is talking about genuine change—"all human relations have
shifted"—but all her examples, social, historical, and class-bound as
they are, demonstrate the basic cultural continuity of her stance.
Character, it appears, may be shaped and altered from within—not
easily, perhaps, and not utterly, but nevertheless. Character in life,
as in novels, is a human (though probably not an individual) creation. For Woolf, the key to this kind of change is *convention*. The
novelists of Bennett's generation, she says,

developed a technique of novel-writing which suits their purpose;
they have made tools and established conventions which do their
business. But those tools are not our tools, and that business is not
our business. For us those conventions are ruin, those tools are
death. (16)

Here, of course, Woolf is concerned with novelistic conventions; but
again, precisely as she does in her discussion of character, she blurs
the distinction between art and life:

A convention in writing is not much different from a convention in
manners. Both in life and in literature it is necessary to have some
means of bridging the gulf between the hostess and her unknown
guest on the one hand, the writer and his unknown reader on the
other. . . . The writer must get in touch with his reader by putting

before him something which he recognizes, which therefore stimulates his imagination, and makes him willing to co-operate in the far more difficult business of intimacy. And it is of the highest importance that this common meeting-place should be reached easily, almost instinctively, in the dark, with one's eyes shut. (17)

The novelist's conventions, like those of the "hostess," are ultimately communal, insofar as they both govern and serve human relationships. And in a time when, as Woolf says, "all human relations have shifted," conventions inevitably alter.

All this ought to be obvious; times change, style changes. But the modernist period, Woolf's genteel account notwithstanding, has about it a quality of urgency not addressed in "Mr. Bennett and Mrs. Brown." The reasons are well documented. Cultural mutations that had been gestating since the Renaissance—scientific, theological, philosophical, technological, psychological, social—bore such strange fruit between 1910 and 1931 that the western world had every right to its conviction that it would never be the same again. No one understood this situation more clearly, or felt it more fully, than Woolf. In *The Common Reader*, she describes how "In the vast catastrophe of the European war our emotions had to be broken up for us, and put at an angle from us, before we could allow ourselves to feel them in poetry or fiction" (Howard xiii). But the self, that curious human character who is in some ratio partly a natural thing and partly an artifact, lives for Woolf in a present that is always wonderfully and grievously the present and no more than that. In *Mrs. Dalloway*, a book whose every word is subtly, tragically darkened by the shadow of the war, Peter Walsh thinks,

> For this is the truth about our soul, . . . our self, who fish-like inhabits deep seas and plies among obscurities threading her way between the boles of giant weeds, over sun-flickered spaces and on and on into gloom, cold, deep, inscrutable; suddenly she shoots to the surface and sports on the wind-wrinkled waves; that is, has a positive need to brush, scrape, kindle herself, gossiping. What did the Government mean . . . to do about India? (161)

Politics? The genius of the sovereign self? For Woolf the writer, as she records in her diary, the problem boils down to this: "I have to create the whole thing afresh for myself each time. Probably all writers now are in the same boat. It is the penalty we pay for breaking with tradition" (Howard ix). Convention is no mere empty mannerism; linked to the essence of character, it is a matter of life and death. This is how perilous the issue of style has become, how bound up with the character of the writer, the character of the written.

Character is not a term in general or incisive use by critics of lyric poetry; it belongs more to traditional criticism of epic, fiction, and drama when it applies to writing, and to moral philosophy when it applies to life. Yet why this should be so is not altogether clear. Lyric poems project characters as insistently as do these other modes, even if the character should be as nosing and fishlike a self as, say, the speaker of Adrienne Rich's "Diving into the Wreck," or as vast and affable a surface-shooter as the "I" of Whitman's "Song of Myself." And if readers make the mistake, as poems often encourage them to do, of imagining that poems are utterances direct from the hearts of the poets themselves, then they are concerning themselves more with the moral-philosophical sense of character than with the literary—sometimes harmlessly, sometimes fruitfully, sometimes chaotically.

Ezra Pound, as is well known, got round this difficulty by coining his own word for the character who sits at the heart of a lyric poem, its center of consciousness: *persona*, a word he borrowed from the Greek for *mask*. The New Critics, following his lead, made a hard and fast distinction between the realms of art and life; but poststructuralism has called the distinction into question again, reintroducing history, biography, autobiography, politics, and other "extraliterary" concerns into criticism. *Character*, for critics of poetry, has remained a lost continent. But its roots are as respectably Greek as those of Pound's *persona*: *kharakter*, a tool for engraving, the marks made by that tool; hence, *character* as a mark of the pen, a letter of the alphabet, precedes *character* as an attribute of the self, or as hero of an epic, member of the cast of a play, focus of a novel. And in this double root sense, as the inscriber and the inscribed—as tool, as engraving, as writing—*kharakter* seems as well suited to postmodern theoretical agendas as *persona* to those of modernism.

Convention might likewise profitably be defined in its root sense, as a coming together, the zone within which *kharakter* meets character—where host meets guest, where writer meets reader, where Achilles meets Odysseus, where the tool of inscribing meets the medium of inscription—and where each of these, by coming into relatedness, becomes what it is. Like the shape of the table at the Paris Peace Talks, like the terms of the Geneva Convention, such a zone must be a site of continual negotiation and renegotiation; all roles and relationships must be defined and redefined.

Poetry in America, as elsewhere, has negotiated many treaties. But, perhaps because American poetry is so young, its conventions have never been clearly settled, its character never precisely determined. At least since Emerson, American poetry has been in question; at least since Longfellow, it has had its professional diplomats; at least since Whitman and Dickinson, it has had its stark polarities. But at no time was the tension so great, the argument so loud, as in the period between 1910 and 1931.

What was as stake? No less than everything poetry is. Every term, every attitude, every definition, every myth was suddenly up for grabs. Once again, American poetry was out to create itself, and the dream of American modernism in its most extreme form was that American poetry could do so *ex nihilo*—not because American poets were gods, even "gods in ruin" as Emerson said, but because there was nothing there to create poetry *from*. Discontinuity: in this version of the modernist dream, or nightmare, there was no American past, no metaphysic, no rhetoric, no overarching aesthetic, that could inform poetry, or anything else worth informing. This myth was no more true than any other; few subscribed to it completely, and none with perfect consistency for very long. It reveals its own root contradiction in the very fact of its Romantic essence; American Romanticism has always maintained the oxymoronic tradition of being without a tradition. But the effect of the modernist myth was, as everyone knows, profound, simultaneously liberating and enervating.

Clearly, the modernism described by this myth is the modernism of Pound, Eliot, Stein, Stevens, and others, writers who, one way or another, abandoned America in order to write its poems. But there was another kind of American modernism, as fully "modern" as the other, that was more overtly local, more populist, less aesthetically radical. This was the modernism of New England and the prairie, of Ohio and California; Robert Frost is its signal patriarch and the school of John Crowe Ransom its scribes and pharisees, mainstream New Criticism and agrarianism the cathedrals of its orthodox wing, Robinson Jeffers its Jeremiah, William Carlos Williams its John the Baptist, Countee Cullen its black Christ, Marianne Moore its most incisive technician of the sacred, Randall Jarrell its most genial assassin. And its influence continues: Hart Crane and Allen Ginsberg are its princes of darkness, Elizabeth Bishop its subtlest agnostic, Robert Lowell its bastard godchild, Adrienne Rich its most splendid apostate and heretic, Philip Levine its lightning bolt. But farther back in the penumbra, increasingly out of sight, are other figures, important and even crucial players, advocates, teachers, innovators—failures if visibility is, as it must on some level be, the signature of success, but nevertheless indispensably part of the fierce polemic struggle that propelled and consumed American poetry in the first third of this century—indispensably part of the story.

Put simply, the struggle in poetry between 1910 and 1931 was elemental. It involved three matters: what poetry could (and should) include; what it could (and should) exclude; what it could (and crucially had to) laugh offstage. The first can be called, straightforwardly, *the poetic*: what is fit substance for poetry in terms of subject, craft, language, and every other consideration. The second is *the unpoetic*, that which is beyond the pale, that which poetry cannot and will not incorporate, to which it is even oblivious (and if the American myth since Whitman is that poetry has permission to be about anything at all, the fact is that it has not yet contained everything, and never will). The third—and for modernism the most interesting, and arguably the most crucial—is *the "poetic"*: what the word *poetic* comes to mean when it is said, as it most often is among us now, with irony. The "poetic" consists of everything poetry once was and now no longer can be—everything clichéd, everything sentimental, everything old-fashioned, outworn, super-seded; in short, everything that can be perceived as habitual, inau-thentic, inept in those particularly damning ways that "bad" poetry can be defined as inept.

At any moment, in the work of any poet or in the poetry of any people, these three boundaries define the area of effective conven-tion, the zone within which poets and poems and readers meet and mutually inscribe the *character* of their rapprochement. The terms are insistently fluid; every poet and all poetry must negotiate and renegotiate them. But obviously, for poetry that is manifestly "mod-ern," insistently of a present that is self-avowedly unlike any present has ever been, the concept of the "poetic" must take on more significance than in other periods. Modernism is in fact most poetically radical in defining the "poetic." What modernism allows poetry to include and what it utterly excludes, what it champions and what it ignores, are fundamentally traditional: novelty, intelli-gence, authenticity, cosmopolitanism, concentrated craft, aestheti-cism, angst—none of this is news. But in the realm of the "poetic," the High Modernists were innovative geniuses who turned ironic laughter into a revolutionary technique.

One of the most famous—because it is one of the best—stories about the young Ezra Pound concerns his showing poems to Ford Madox Ford in 1911. The story has often been told, but no one has ever told it better than Pound himself:

> [Ford] felt the errors of contemporary style to the point of rolling
> (physically, and if you look at it as a mere superficial snob, ridicu-
> lously) on the floor of his temporary quarters in Gissen when my
> third volume displayed me trapped, fly-papered, gummed and
> strapped down in a jejune provincial effort to learn, *mehercule*, the
> stilted language that then passed for "good English" in the arthritic
> milieu that held control of the respected British critical circles. . . .
>
> And that roll saved me at least two years, perhaps more. It sent
> me back to my own proper effort, namely, toward using the living
> tongue. (*Selected Prose* 461–62)

So exquisitely comical, so "poetic," did Ford find Pound's "jejune
provincial" poems that he could not contain himself; his gesture
continues to resonate, in legend, in pedagogy, in poetry, right down
to the present.

Pound got the point with a vengeance. In retrospect, he understood perfectly what was "poetic" in the poems Ford fell on the floor
mocking; he also understood how important a lesson Ford's laughter had taught him, how much time it had saved. This moment in
Gissen became a sort of primal scene for Pound, the ultimate workshop experience; he reiterated it again and again in his criticism,
championing a "revolution in taste" that would not abolish everything "poetic" from poetry but would keep it always at arm's length,
where it could form one pole of the field of tension poetry had to be.
The presence of the "poetic," for Pound, was indispensable. If he
had succeeded in banishing it entirely into the realm of the sheerly
unpoetic, he would have committed aesthetic suicide. To be at his
best, Pound always needed something to laugh off.

But if the character of Pound's poetry is founded in part on the
laughter of that "character" Ford Madox Ford, it is founded equally
on another laugh, one more distant, perhaps, but larger and more
resonant. "I say I have not seen a single writer, artist, lecturer, or
what not," Walt Whitman wrote in *Democratic Vistas* (1871),

> that has confronted the voiceless but ever erect and active, pervad-
> ing, underlying will and typical aspiration of the land, in a spirit

kindred to itself. Do you call those genteel little creatures American poets? Do you term that perpetual, pistareen, paste-pot work, American art, American drama, taste, verse? I think I hear, echoed as from some mountain-top afar in the west, the scornful laugh of the Genius of these States. (34–35)

Whitman names no names in this essay; it is not necessary that he do so, because he is talking about all American art, except perhaps (and only perhaps) his own. The thoroughly radical nature of Whitman's project is a given; he is out to reinvent America from its artists up.

> Our fundamental want to-day in the United States . . . is of a class, and the clear idea of a class, of native authors, literatuses, far different, far higher in grade, than any yet known, sacerdotal, modern, fit to cope with our occasions, lands, permeating the whole mass of American mentality, taste, belief, breathing into it a new breath of life. . . . The priest departs, the divine literatus comes. Never was anything more wanted than, today, and here in the States, the poet of the modern is wanted, or the great literatus of the modern. (5–6)

For Whitman, anything less than the "divine literatus" was a joke and an affront: a mockery of poetry, of the manifest largeness of the role of the poet, of the American nation, and hence of humankind. But it was also an affront against the modern. As much as Pound or any of the other post-1910 proselytizers, Whitman demanded that American poets be "sacerdotal, modern"; *Democratic Vistas* is as much a manifesto of modernism as Pound's essay "Patria Mea," which in many ways—not least in its loose epigrammatic structure and its tendency toward outrageous, unsubstantiatedly authoritarian pronouncement—imitates it.

Of course, there are fundamental and profound differences between the modern as Whitman sees it and the modern as defined by Pound. The philosophical and aesthetic differences are enormous and more or less obvious; the difference in their character can be grasped quickly by coming to understand the differences in what

can be laughed off and how. For Whitman, there are two kinds of
laughter, one apocalyptic and one contemptible. Describing the mal-
aise of America in the 1870s, he writes,

> Genuine belief seems to have left us. The underlying principles of
> the States are not honestly believ'd in . . . nor is humanity itself
> believ'd in. What penetrating eye does not everywhere see through
> the mask? . . . We live in an atmosphere of hypocrisy throughout.
> The men believe not in the women, nor the women in the men. A
> scornful superciliousness rules in literature. The aim of all the
> *littérateurs* is to find something to make fun of. (11–12)

The laughter of the littérateurs, clearly, is not the same as "the
scornful laugh of the Genius of these States"; the one belongs to the
"genteel little creature" the literatus becomes when he or she turns
into the littérateur, and the other belongs in typically undefined
Whitmanic fashion to the body politic or the zeitgeist. The difference between the literatus and the littérateur and their different
modes of laughter is precisely the difference between Whitman's
poetic and his *"poetic"*; the one defines what poetry has to be, the
other defines what it must, through the scorn of the "Genius of
these States," laugh offstage. For Whitman, this difference is precisely a matter of character in the strictest sense: how poetry inscribes the people who must in turn inscribe the poet who inscribes
the poem.

For Pound, on the other hand, the literatus has become an un-
thinkable absurdity; the littérateur is all that remains, the only possibility. But the littérateur must therefore be astonishingly good at being a littérateur, not just a good technician but the best possible
technician, the best of all possible technicians, a genius not of "the
whole mass of American mentality, taste, belief," but of craft, of
knowledge, of literature itself. Where for Whitman the ultimate authority to which the poet appeals, that which inscribes the character
of the poet, is "the Genius of these States," for Pound it is what he
comes to call Kulchur, the most serious joke of them all.

Thus, for Pound, Whitman—though the greatest of American poets—is scarcely a poet at all. As spokesman for "the Genius of these States," Whitman became, as far a Pound was concerned, a "Reflex" rather than an artist:

> [W]e had to ourselves Whitman, "The Reflex," who left us a human document, for you cannot call a man an artist until he shows himself in some degree master of the forces which beat upon him.
> ("Patria Mea" 114)

If this is a judgment against Whitman and Whitman's brand of modernism, it is an uneasy judgment. On the very next page of "Patria Mea," Pound acknowledges the essentially reflexive nature of art: "the poet," he says, "is a sort of steam-gauge, voltameter, a set of pipes for thermometric and barometric divination" (115). And in "What I Feel about Walt Whitman," a quick assessment written in 1909 (unpublished until 1955), Pound gives a wonderfully clear statement of his ambivalence toward Whitman—an ambivalence that never altered, though this particular formulation of it predates Ford Madox Ford's apocalyptic mockery:

> [Whitman] is America. His crudity is an exceeding great stench, but it is America. He is the hollow place in the rock that echoes with his time. . . . I read him (in many parts) with acute pain, but when I write of certain things I find myself using his rhythms. . . . The vital part of my message, taken from the sap and fibre of America, is the same as his. . . . Mentally I am a Walt Whitman who has learned to wear a collar and a dress shirt (although at times inimical to both).
> (145)

One impulse at the foundation of Pound's project, though he never expressed it, is to conflate the literatus and the littérateur, to make their missions, and their ironies, one potent force. "It seems to me," he writes, "I should like to drive Whitman into the old world. I sledge, he drill—and to scourge America with all the old beauty. (For Beauty is an accusation)" ("What I Feel" 146). Pound is everywhere concerned with *character*, from his obsession with the ideogram to his repeated demand for an American Renaissance. "The thesis I defend," he declares in "Patria Mea," "is: that American has a chance for Renaissance and that certain absurdities in the manners of American action are, after all, things of the surface and not of necessity the symptoms of sterility or even of fatal disease" (102). The largest issues of craft and theme must be attended to; but equally the absurdities must be recognized for what they are and obliterated with an irony as powerful and incisive as a rock-drill. "American poetry is bad," he says, "not for a lack of impulse, but because almost no one in that country knows true from false, good from bad" ("Patria Mea" 127).

True/false, good/bad: are these ethical or aesthetic categories? Purposely—as purposely as Woolf's blurring of the distinction between character in fiction and character in life—they are rendered both. And for Pound, often if not always, the truest test of the worth of an artist as well as the worth of art is whether he, she, or it can stand the caustic force of the most serious and insistent laughter. Paradoxically, this turns out as often as not to be a grim and even cruel criterion; sometimes, too, the test rebounds on itself, and Pound himself looks more foolish than the object of his derision. His attempt to parody Whitman, for instance, falls flat: invoking what he calls Whitman's delight in "rejoic[ing] in being Whitman," he writes,

> Whitman is the voice of one who saith:
>
> Lo, behold, I eat water-melons. When I eat water-melons the world
>   eats water-melons through me.
> When the world eats water-melons, I partake of the world's water-
>   melons.
> The bugs,
> The worms,
> The negroes, etc.,
> Eat water-melons; all nature eats water-melons.

Those eidolons and particles of the Cosmos
Which do not now partake of water-melons
Will at some future time partake of water-melons.
Praised be Allah or Ramanathanath Krishna!

. . . Whitman, having decided that it is disgraceful to be ashamed,
rejoices in having attained nudity.

(*Spirit* 168–69)

Unfortunately for Pound, this parody, in both style and substance,
sounds more like Pound than like Whitman: too much so for it to do
other than rebound on its author (compare the offhanded racism of
"The negroes, etc." to the naïveté of Lindsay's attempt at mytholo-
gizing "all the panorama of the Negro race" in "The Congo"). Such
moments reveal, on the one hand, the relentless force of Pound's
desire to "scourge America," and on the other the limits of his
means. Laughter is a potent weapon in the poetry wars, but writing
conceived with sufficient impure toughness simply shrugs it off.

Vachel Lindsay is responsible for a body of poetry that is nothing if
not idiosyncratic. It partakes very obviously of the mainstream tradition of Romanticism, thematically influenced most markedly by the
gnostic branch thereof (Blake and Poe) but also by the more orthodox Romanticism of Milton (it is to the Romantic side of Milton that
Lindsay responds), Wordsworth, Keats, and—as problematically as
Pound—Whitman. It would be easy to write off Lindsay as an
awkward late Romantic, the sort of figure a less intelligent Yeats
might have become if he had remained stuck in the earliest mode of
his Celtic Twilight phase; but fundamental elements of some of
Lindsay's poems belie such a view. Insofar as he comes to take as his
subject matter certain aspects of his contemporary world that other
poets might have regarded as essentially unpoetic, insofar as he
struggles to create a voice infused with the rhythms of his moment,
Lindsay's poems are as modern—in their own strange way as modern*ist*—as anyone's.

At the peak of his career he was famous—and to the extent that he is still remembered, he is notorious—for the exaggerated musicality of his poems. Virginia Woolf—who one is, well, *dumbstruck* to discover actually wrote about Lindsay—describes this quality of his work very accurately:

> His gift is rhythmical, one suspects, rather than verbal, until further discoveries make it wise to suspend that judgment for a time. With the rhythm goes, in many of the poems, a queer suggestion of instrumental music. Here, one feels, the cymbals should crash; here sounds the brass; here the tambourines; and here and here should be dancing and swaying in time. The audience should take their measure from the poet, who, as he recites, stands in the centre of a circle with his feet wide apart, so that he may turn on his heel, speaking rapidly, his hands moving, his voice "changing in pace, rhythm and volume, but never in tone." ("An American Poet" 168–69, quoted in Lindsay, *General William Booth*)

Woolf then quotes the first stanza of Lindsay's "General William Booth Enters into Heaven," the poem instrumental, as it were, in launching the phenomenon of his fame when it appeared as the lead piece in the January 1913 issue of Harriet Monroe's *Poetry* magazine:

> (*Bass drum beaten loudly.*)
> Booth led boldly with his big bass drum—
> (Are you washed in the blood of the Lamb?)
> The Saints smiled gravely and they said: "He's come."
> (Are you washed in the blood of the Lamb?)
> Walking lepers followed, rank on rank,
> Lurching bravos from the ditches dank,
> Drabs from the alleyways and drug fiends pale—
> Minds still passion-ridden, soul-powers frail:—
> Vermin-eaten saints with moldy breath,
> Unwashed legions with the ways of Death—
> (Are you washed in the blood of the Lamb?)
>
>   (*General William Booth* 148)

What readers in 1913 found so striking about this poem may not be easy to see at first glance. Monroe herself was immediately certain of "General William Booth" and of its author; she wrote that Lindsay "represents a tendency much richer and more indigenous than the imagists. . . . His roots run deep into the past of American literature: Mark Twain and [James Whitcomb] Riley and Brer-Rabbit Harris were his collateral relatives" (Carpenter 212). Her certainty as she expresses it here goes to the Americanness of Lindsay's work as it can be identified as traditional; she seems less attuned to its more radical qualities. Indeed, in the end Monroe's favorite Lindsay poem was the far less adventurous though arguably more mellifluous "The Chinese Nightingale," which she published in 1915 and to which she gave *Poetry*'s annual prize that year—over Eliot's "The Love Song of J. Alfred Prufrock," to Pound's everlasting horror and disgust. He had written to Monroe, "If your committee don't make the award to Eliot, God only knows what slough of ignominy they will fall into . . . ! ! ! ! ! ! ! !" (Carpenter 262), a jeremiad that earned Eliot no more than an honorable mention in the contest.

Pound had already gone on record about Lindsay:

Vachel Lindsay's "General William Booth Enters into Heaven" appeared in [*Poetry*] during 1913, and Carl Sandburg had a sequence of his "Chicago poems" printed in the issue for March 1914. Ezra did not notice either for some time, and when he eventually observed Lindsay he simply said, "Oh gawd! ! !" (Carpenter 212)

In 1918 he carried his assault on Lindsay farther. As Humphrey Carpenter tells us, Pound published in the *Little Review*

a forty-eight-line "poem" in imitation of Lindsay's "General William Booth," written (he said) in precisely four minutes and thirty-one seconds:

>Whoop-golly-ip Zopp, bob BIP! !
>I'm Mr. Lindsay with the new sheep-dip,
>I'm a loud-voiced yeller, I'm a prancing preacher,
>Gawd's in his heaven! I'm the *real* High Reacher. (212)

The accuracy of this pastiche (vastly more effective than the Whitman parody) is undeniable; Pound has nailed not only the sound of Lindsay's poem, but its character—that is, not General Booth, the character at the center of dramatic focus of the poem, but the visionary/oratorical character of its center of consciousness. Pound comically retains the rhythms of Lindsay's poem but inverts its rhetorical method in order to emphasize a character more or less invisible in the original: the "prancing preacher" narrator, the "real High Reacher" who puts himself above even "Gawd." If Pound finds Lindsay technically suspect here—and he does—he reveals Lindsay the visionary at least equally suspect dramatically, and his wicked little parody works to undermine both authorities simultaneously.

Amy Lowell, too, got in her licks, though in a more good-natured and less devastating manner than Pound. In her anonymously published doggerel poem *A Critical Fable*, an update of her ancestor James Russell Lowell's *The Bigelow Papers*, Lowell wrote parodic descriptions of a whole range of her contemporary poets. Of Lindsay, she wrote,

> He's a composite choir, whether shouting or chanting,
> Whoever's heard once must admit to a haunting
> Nostalgia to hear him again. It's enchanting.
> A Sunday-school orator, plus inspiration,
> The first ballad-singer, bar none, of the Nation. . . .
> An odd, antic fellow, but if you insist
> On the unvarnished truth, a sublime egotist. . . .
> He's a sort of mad xylophone, twinkling his bells
> Before all the doors of the thirty-six Hells.
>   . . . He's astoundingly mystic
> Even when he purports to be most naturalistic,
> A queer ancient trait we may call Judaistic,
> Engraft on a style which is pure Methodistic.
> He is always attempting to fathom his soul,
> But he cannot get hold of a long enough pole.

As he uses an ancient one which he inherited,
Perhaps, after all, his failure is merited. (40, 41)

Woolf's response to Lindsay is a carefully balanced equivocation. It appears that she does not care much for his poems, and yet she is unwilling to say flatly that they are not good; he is, after all, an American, and therefore just possibly incomprehensible. She refers first to Nichols's description of Lindsay and his performance style in the introduction to *General William Booth* and then sidles up to a consideration of the poems themselves:

You see that Mr. Nichols is much impressed by the size, the sunburn, the vitality; this man [Lindsay] writes poetry, yet he is much like a farm labourer to look at. The Englishman is disposed to think well of Mr. Lindsay's poems on that account. Then he finds that Mr. Lindsay tours the country reciting his poetry for a living, and that has proved to Mr. Nichols "once and for all that poetry has too long been manufactured and read in the study; that the enmity between poetry and the populace has its origin in *print*; whereby poetry has lost its 'springiness'; has become a thing too much of the eye; a cult of solitude . . . the refuge of preciosity in those folk who have made of poetry a retreat from life and not an explanation and justification in beauty of life." There you have the Englishman doing what it is so fatally easy for the English of the present day to do—worshipping vitality, divesting himself of culture, trying to get away, to get back, to forget, to renew.

But we can be generous without being obsequious. There is every reason to believe that America can bring something new to literature; it is high time, we may add, that America did. Nobody is so certain of an enthusiastic welcome in England as a true American poet; directly the figure or the shadow of one appears above the horizon all eyes are shaded and turned in his direction. What hopes are there then, of Nicholas Vachel Lindsay? Naturally, inevitably perhaps, the answer is not a single jubilant hail! but one that takes time and thought to deliver; one of the qualified kind. (167)

As she often does, Woolf touches the heart of the matter when she fixes on Nichols's discussion of text versus performance. It is precisely on the perilous boundary between these two modes that Lindsay insistently places his poems; such power as his work has, its fragility, the whole character of his career, arises out of the resulting tension.

Woolf was not the only critic to explore this borderline in Lindsay's work. In 1914 a review of *The Congo and Other Poems, General William Booth Enters into Heaven and Other Poems,* and *Adventures While Preaching the Gospel of Beauty,* signed R.S.B., began this way:

> You must hear Mr. Lindsay recite his own "Congo," his body tense and swaying, his hands keeping time like an orchestral leader to his own rhythms, his tone changing color in response to noise and savage imagery of the lines, the riotous picture of the negro mind set against the weird background of the primitive Congo, the "futurist" phrases crashing through the scene like a glorious college yell,—you must hear this yourself, and learn what an arresting, exciting person this new indigenous Illinois poet is. He has a theory of his work, which Miss Monroe has supported in *Poetry,* that he is carrying back the half-spoken, half-chanted singing of the American vaudeville stage to its old Greek precedent of the rhapsodist's lyric, where the poet was composer and reciter in one. . . . [O]ne's imagination begins to run away with the idea of this Greek rhapsodist-vaudeville stage, where one could get the color and the smash of American life interpreted on a higher and somewhat more versatile plane than is now presented. . . . The explicitly poetical stage directions which accompany these poems "to be read aloud or chanted" initiate the reader at once into the art, and rather spoil him for the tame business of reading. ("Sincerity in the Making" 26)

"You must hear this yourself," R.S.B. insists, as if the poems on the page are inadequate to convey the effects he describes. There is much that is indirectly revealing in this little passage—its naïve racism, its extolling of the "glorious college yell," its straightforward acceptance of Lindsay's "stage directions" as purely *non*textual in impact (what exactly does a performer do with such a direction as "a philosophical pause," or even more mysterious, "All the 'o' sounds very golden"?). Still, already in 1914 R.S.B. does perceive the central controlling mode of Lindsay's career: the "Greek rhapsodist-vaudeville stage." Lindsay himself named this phenomenon "the Higher Vaudeville," and it became, from March 1914 onward, the foundation of his fame.

Of Lindsay's performance style, as Paul Gray comments, "only a few scratchy recordings" remain, and "we have no way of knowing what it was like to be present at a Lindsay performance, but the effect left few untouched" (221). Gray then cites Eleanor Ruggles's account of Lindsay onstage:

> "As Vachel Lindsay came forward on a stage," one critic was to write, "the force of his personality brought an immediate sense of expectancy in his audience." Another spoke of his "electric presence. . . . He set the throng on fire." . . . The communion was intoxicating. Those who never saw him in his handling of an audience never knew the whole man; he worked them up, led them row against row, aisle against aisle, the floor against the balcony. It was self-intoxicating. (Ruggles 237, 243)

"Self-intoxicating" is an odd and telling phrase—the self, every self present, is intoxicated? Lindsay is intoxicated by his own "carrying on in public"? Lindsay's performances may have been ecstatic (these descriptions are positively Pentecostal), but they were also carefully choreographed. Balz Engler gives a more particular description of Lindsay's "Higher Vaudeville" techniques, quoting from a brochure Lindsay had privately printed and sent to his performance venues in advance of his own arrival:

> First, "a hymn of ballad of long standing somewhat parallel in thought" is chosen as "the natural meter." . . . Second, tone color, "imitative verbal music," is extensively used, supporting communi-

cation on the affective level. Finally, the chanting of lines in a manner reminiscent of Gregorian chant adds a ritualistic element to the experience of sharing.

As we know from reports, Lindsay also invited his audiences to participate actively by clapping their hands, nodding and shaking their heads at certain points, and by repeating lines or by chanting refrains. This physical involvement helped create a community of those liberated from the passivity typical of such occasions. A community would then be more receptive to the vision that followed the Higher Vaudeville portion of the programme. (31)

Written accounts of such events clearly leave much to the imagination. Responding to Robert Nichols's textual version of Lindsay the rhapsodist-minstrel in action, Virginia Woolf is a bit less carried away than either Nichols or R.S.B. (There is no evidence that Woolf ever attended one of Lindsay's performances, though because he made several reading tours of England, it is possible that she did.) The measured ambivalence of her judgment—"His gift is rhythmical, one suspects, rather than verbal, until further discoveries make it wise to suspend that judgment for a time"—is perfectly plain. "Perhaps the undoubted effectiveness of his rhythms," she goes on to say, "is also the result of youth"—though in 1920 when this review was published, Lindsay was forty-one.

> A sophisticated ear would fight shy of them. . . . No great strain is laid upon the intellect; the strain is on the emotions. If you stop to examine the lines separately, none is specially memorable. . . . But however we rate Mr. Lindsay's worth as a poet, it is impossible, though it may well be unfair, not to seize upon those strains in him which appear to us, rightly or wrongly, the proof of his American birth—his simplicity; his moral earnestness; his primitive love of rhythm. . . . We look into the bubbling cauldron from which something shapely of a new kind may one of these days emerge. (169–70)

These are the characteristics one *wishes* to discover in an American: youth, simplicity, earnestness, and above all *primitivity* (precisely, in fact, what an American of the 1920s wishes to discover in an African). Woolf may be a shade unsure of the value of these attributes, but she recognizes them as given in the consideration of the work of an American poet. Nichols, she thinks, may be a little too sheerly British in his unquestioning appreciation of the "primitive" Lindsay; but neither is she willing to suggest bluntly there may be nothing to his claims. Perhaps sophistication is overrated after all.

The demand for the primitive, the elemental, in American poetry was equally insistent among Americans. In 1918 Max Eastman made an unfavorable comparison of Whitman to Poe on the basis of the relative "primitivity" of the poetry:

> Walt Whitman was not really playful and childlike enough to go back to nature. His poetry was less primitive and savage than it was superhuman and sublime. His emotions were as though they came to him through a celestial telescope. There is something more properly savage—something at least truly barbarous—in a poem like Poe's "Bells." And in Poe's insistence upon "Beauty" as the sole legitimate province of the poem—beauty, which he defines as a special and dispassionate "excitement of the soul"—he is nearer to the mood of the snake dance. ("American Ideals of Poetry, II" 223)

If this argument has an odd ring today—who among us would seriously place Poe's "Bells" above "Song of Myself" or find in it an ecstasy more genuine?—such questions were of crucial importance to Eastman and to many other American artists and intellectuals for whom American writing, American culture, and particularly American poetry had come to a critical crossroad. At stake was the relation of poetry to its audience, a matter regarding which Eastman had strong opinions.

> The opposition of these two characters and attitudes [Whitman's and Poe's] is complete. Upon the one side a vast preoccupation with human meaning and morals, with health and the common reality and love and democracy, a grand contempt for beauty and for the

effort to attract or gratify a reader with "verbal melody," a contempt
for everything that savors of deliberate technique in art. Upon the
other side also contempt—contempt like a piece of cold analytical
steel for every pretense that the technique of art is not deliberate,
that poets are not seeking to attract and gratify, that truth or moral
or meaning instead of beauty is the portent of a poem—a disposi-
tion to seek beauty in unique and even unhealthy places, a lonely
aristocratic heart of pain, and a preoccupation with "verbal melody"
never before or since equaled in poetry. . . . Now, it is not merely an
accident, or a reflection upon American or upon human nature, that
Walt Whitman, with all his yearnings over the average American
and his offering of priesthood and poetry to the people, should
remain the poet of a rather esoteric few, whereas Poe—even with
the handful of poems he wrote—may be said to be acceptable to the
generality of men. . . . For the emotions and the meanings of Walt
Whitman's poetry *are* the emotions and meanings that interest
simple and thoughtful people who have leisure to feel. His realiza-
tions of life would be acceptable and be honored, as much at least as
great art is ever honored, by the "divine average," if they were con-
veyed as Poe's were in vessels of light which would make them
objective and from which they might brim over with excess of sub-
jective meaning and emotion. ("Ideals, I" 191–92)

The core of Eastman's complex and doomed argument is accessibil-
ity, as it relates to objectivity vs. subjectivity on the one hand and to
a specific kind of musicality on the other. For Eastman, as for the
neoformalist poets of the 1980s, traditional meter is the cynosure,
the point of technique where these two arguments meet. According
to this argument, so-called free verse is essentially arbitrary and sub-
jective and therefore inaccessible to Eastman's "divine average,"
whereas the conventions of traditional rhyme and meter provide (exactly how he does not say) a known and common ground:

A mature science of rhythm might be imagined to stride into the
room where these poets are discussing the musical values of their

verse, seize two or three of the most "free" and subtle among them, lock them into separate sound-proof chambers, and allow them to read one of their favorite passages into the ear of a machine designed to record in spatial outline the pulsations of vocal accent. It is safe to assert that there would be less identity in the actual pulsations recorded than if the same two were reading a passage of highly wrought English prose. . . . [Whitman] wanted his poetry to sound with nature and the untutored heart of humanity. It was in the radiance of this desire that he spoke of rhythmical prose as a "vast diviner heaven" toward which poetry would move in its future development in America. Prose seemed to him diviner because it seemed more simple, more large with candor and directness. But here again a cool and clear science will show that his nature led him in a contrary direction from its ideal. (223–24)

Eastman, with his paradoxical double emphasis on the scientific and on the primitive, sounds in the end like an anthropologist who would make graphs of shamanistic ecstasy. Hence, perhaps, comes his attraction to Poe, who combines "cold analytic steel" with what Eastman insistently calls both "exquisite" and "savage."

Hence also his attraction—referred to directly in a footnote, but invoked in the notion of a "mature science of rhythm"—to the work of Dr. William Morrison Patterson, a professor of English at Columbia University engaged in an acoustic study of human response to rhythm. In soundproof rooms in the departments of psychology and of physics, Patterson set up "instruments for transforming by means of a diaphragm and small mirrors, the vibrations of the voice into vibrations of a light-ray, susceptible of being photographed" (103), and conducted various experiments aimed especially at discovering a scientifically objective and quantifiable answer to the presiding question "What is prose and what is verse?" (ix). No less a personage than Amy Lowell submitted her voice to "the ear of [Patterson's] machine designed to record in spatial outline the pulsations of vocal accent"—with inconclusive results, however politely Patterson stated them:

Miss Amy Lowell's generous readiness to deliver, in the author's photographing laboratory, readings of what she considers typical *vers libre*, has resulted in objective measurements which indicate interesting progressive changes in the temporal intervals from one chief accent to another, but nothing, as yet, which indicates a difference in *kind* between the "cadances" of *vers libre* and those of emotive prose. . . . Miss Lowell delivers her *vers libre* with much more swing and vim than one commonly hears in prose, but surely all particularly vigorous prose, if it is to be valued as a fit medium for vigorous thought and feeling, must also be thus delivered. (xii–xiii)

Patterson's interest in rhythm ranges freely among many types of rhythmic human productions: poetry, fiction, music. He is continually frustrated in his efforts to make clean distinctions between human responses to these different media; individual subjects seem finally overwhelmingly inconsistent in their capacity to hear, reproduce, or create rhythms. In one forlorn paragraph, he notes that "by one observer a short group of words was found susceptible of being marked for stress, pitch, duration, and weight, in seven hundred ways!" (96). So much for the "science" of meter. But what impels Patterson's studies, and what fills his book with curious melancholy charm, is his continual rediscovery of the fundamental importance of rhythmic experience in human life, and his quasi-scientific eulogizing of the poverty of "civilized" existence in its awareness of this fact:

The music of contemporary savages, such as that of the Kwakiutl . . . taunts us with a lost art of rhythm. Modern sophistication has inhibited many native instincts, and the mere fact that our conventional dignity usually forbids us to sway our bodies or to tap our feet when we hear effective music, has deprived us of unsuspected pleasures. Certain it is that the facility of the American Indian in the execution of syncopating rhythms is matched in most of us by a thoroughly blunted process, characterized by hesitation and awkwardness. . . . [S]peaking of the music of the Omahas, Fillmore remarks that in "rich variety and complexity of rhythm" it "excels most of our civilized music by a great deal." (xxi, 7)

Patterson may be the first to eulogize the by now well-documented fact that the "new white man" can't dance. However, he is pleased and astonished to discover that with a little basic training in "actual motor performance" (xxi), almost anyone can learn such complex syncopated rhythms as counting five against seven.

> This would all seem to imply, then, that the mysterious awe with which we regard the rhythmic proficiency of some of our American Indians, for instance, may have to be lessened. Our astonishment should be directed, not so much at their having perpetuated what is, after all, a fairly simple trick, as at our own stupidity in losing the trick. (6)

In music, African American artists were already producing powerfully syncopated new forms of music, from gospel to blues to minstrel-vaudeville to jazz—"The rhythmic consciousness in ragtime," Patterson observes, "is tremendous" (4). So-called *vers libre* is the closest viable literary equivalent, abandoning the more regularized and intellectual patterns of traditional meters for what Whitman had already called the "rhythmical prose as a 'vast diviner heaven' toward which poetry would move in its future development in America." If Max Eastman's argument against Whitman seems retrograde now (however insistently reinvoked and echoed by neoformalists), it is because time and certain developments in the culture—among other things, the readmission into culture of a more complex rhythmic background, doubtless owing in large part to African influences—have proved Whitman right. "Prose rhythm," Patterson observed,

> must always be classed as subjective organization of irregular, virtually haphazard, arrangements of sound. The experience, when judged by a standard of excellence, implies a requisite of fitness between thought and movement, in addition to ease and spontaneity. (xxiv)

This observation might serve as well to describe jazz or a good proportion of so-called free verse—certainly Whitman's own. Framed so, Eastman's pitting of Poe and Whitman against each other as polar opposites seems as oversimple as asking the question, "Which is objectively better: the music of Scarlatti, or that of Louis Armstrong?" A strong pluralism makes its own demands on what we talk about when we talk about "taste."

Though he has often been classified, along with Masters and Sandburg, as one of the most direct inheritors of the tradition of Whitman, Vachel Lindsay shares some of Eastman's reservations about Whitman, not least the conviction that Whitman failed in his mission to be the poet of the people, the chanter of democracy. Asked by the editors of the *New Republic* in 1923 to give his opinion of Whitman for a special supplement of that magazine called "Views of American Poetry," Lindsay wrote:

> You ask my opinion about the place of Walt Whitman in American
> Poetry and hero-worship? He is "in my humble opinion" as big a
> poet as his most emphatic admirer makes him out to be. John
> Burroughs and also the latest Thibetan [sic] to discover *Leaves of
> Grass* are right about the book. But Whitman is no hero, and much
> turns on this. Stephen Graham has generally reported me most
> kindly and most generously. But in one place he has me wrong.
> He says I prefer Longfellow to Whitman. No, I prefer Whitman
> to Longfellow. I agree with the whole of Greenwich Village about
> *Leaves of Grass*. I agree with them about Longfellow's poems. But I
> prefer Andrew Jackson to either man, as a "hero." Here I part with
> the Village.
>
> Those who are impatient with the citizens of the U.S.A. for not
> surrendering abjectly to Walt Whitman, and producing an army of
> singers and citizens of the same style, are blaming a people, when
> they should blame one of the habits of art history. Walt Whitman,
> like Milton and Michael Angelo, has the grand style, with all the

fatalities of the grand style for imitators or slavish admirers. . . .
[T]he citizens of the United States do not fall down before Whitman
in poetry as they do before Lincoln in statesmanship. (3, 4)

For Lindsay as for Eastman, Whitman's "failure" is partly a failure of
style, but even more it is one of character. Implicitly responding—as
Eastman does explicitly—to Whitman's famous line "Who touches
this [book] touches a man," Lindsay claims that "Whitman's book
was a masterpiece, but his life was only half that good," and then
goes on to say,

> Whitman, personally, has less real ginger in his life than the Dam-
> aged Souls of Gamaliel Bradford. For courage and style John Ran-
> dolph of Roanoke was a whole lot more of a man; for frankness and
> variety of incident Barnum outshines Whitman, and for thumping
> democracy Benjamin F. Butler is more of an American, with all his
> sins. I can admire a devil—but he must have some salt. I can ad-
> mire also an angel—but he must have some personal lightning. Not
> all the personal tales about Whitman equal the single simple narra-
> tive of John Randolph, fresh from hunting, marching into Congress
> and down the aisle with his hound-dogs in front of him and a dog-
> whip in his hand. (4)

Character, too, one supposes, is partly a matter of taste. Lindsay objects to Whitman at least partly on the grounds that, compared to
the Jacksonian John Randolph and even to P. T. Barnum (!), Whitman is just not American enough, at least not in the way the "divine
average" would use the term. Near the end of this little essay, Lindsay comes at last, self-revealingly, to what he regards as the heart of
the matter. "Whitman," he claims,

> both as a man and a poet—fails in his definition of United States
> democracy, in an essential matter. He has no chivalry. . . . Whitman
> will always survive outside the main line of tradition as a gigantic
> lonely individual. He cannot take the central place, for he has no
> heroines, not even a Juliet nor a "little shop girl." [Edgar Lee

Masters's character] Anne Rutledge is nearer to being our ultimate
sweetheart and the Virgin Mary nearer to being our ultimate Queen
than all the glad Jezebels of Whitman. There is not one valentine in
him. And America is the land of valentines, white lace valentines. (5)

At this point, one may feel justified in echoing Pound's "Oh, gawd!"
Suddenly, in this head-on encounter with Whitman, just at the point
where we might expect to find the true depth of heart of the "primitive" Lindsay, what we discover instead is a sentimentality so complete that it can hardly be credited.

To attempt to do him justice, it is only fair to point out that in
1923—forty-three years old, never married, arguably still a virgin—
Lindsay was in love. His "Virgin Queen" was Elizabeth Mann Wills,
a nineteen-year-old student at Gulf Park College in Mississippi,
where Lindsay was then teaching. This infatuation, which evidently
remained platonic, was a doomed one, and Lindsay seems already to
sense that fact when, in September 1923, soon after writing his essay
on Whitman, he made the following "confession" to Wills in a letter:

So many critics—so many many critics have said to me "Be our Walt
Whitman." . . . They pour all America into my lap and beg me to
sing about it. I cannot. And here is a secret:—Well—I always considered Whitman as a man and a citizen a genius, but a rather crooked
and shabby old man with a streak of perversion. I can forgive this,
but it keeps the American people from finding leadership in him. I
never mention it out loud. But it spoils him as a model for me. . . .
Whitman never saw the America I have seen and loved. The group
of Brownsville neighbors who came in to hear me could total half a
million or a million—if all my audiences were added up these ten
years. And they—my audiences—always evoke the same mood that
was evoked in Brownsville, and always my audience loves me. . . .
And you do not love me half as well as my audiences do.—you do
not understand. . . . Now Whitman in his wildest dreams was only a
pretended troubadour. He sat still in cafes—never such a troubadour for audiences as Bryan or a thousand Chautauqua men. He
was an infinitely more skillful writer than any other American. But I

can beat him as a *troubadour*. My final gift is the thing that robs me of your love, my darling, I can win an audience in five minutes easier than I can win you in five months though I break my heart and pray to God and to you every hour. (*Letters* 297–98)

For Lindsay, in spite of his own pronouncements to the contrary, Whitman was only a *writer*. He was no "troubadour," not one who could stand before enormous audiences and mystically receive, without the effort of earning, their love.

Lindsay reveals here an enormous, indeed insatiable, desire to be loved. In his particularly middle-class American version of the myth, to be loved as a bard is to be loved as an ideal man. Part of his reservation about Whitman is simply homophobic; it is inconceivable to Lindsay that the American people could ever embrace as a "hero" a person such as Whitman, whom he found dismissable as "a shabby old man with a streak of perversion." Part of it, too, has to do with the world as it appears in Whitman's poetry, especially where women are concerned. "There was no Lady Queen in all of Whitman," Lindsay wrote to Wills. "His fat farm-wives sprawl among the cabbages. . . . You would suppose the nation had no *ivory beauty* if you would listen to him" (298). To be the ideal white American male requires, in this high Romantic rendition, the ideal white American woman, the "ivory beauty" under the spell of whose inspiration the poet can sing the America of white lace valentines into being (the overt symbolic fact about ivory being its whiteness, and the covert being that it is stolen from Africa). This pattern is so familiar that it is almost an embarrassment to point it out—except insofar as the character of Lindsay's project is so thoroughly based on it, and insofar as Lindsay seems completely unaware of its dangers and its contradictions.

More than ample evidence, in the poems and elsewhere, demonstrates that Lindsay, however much of a "Poe-crank" he may have been, was much closer to Whitman in his desire to forge a national poetry for America, and thus secure the purity of the American soul. He is very different from both these writers, however, in his straightforward acceptance of the essential goodness of bourgeois Main Street Americanness. Why would anyone expect a good citizen of Springfield to be a barbarian? Chanting from the heart of the white valentine, Lindsay becomes a living demonstration of the unquestioning acceptance of certain hollow values: a prairie combination of the chivalric and the primitive that often turns out to be nothing more than self-intoxicated self-projection. "No one is going to cure us of the worship of women who are good and beautiful, by any kind of silly theory, even though it be from the latest medical book. No doctor will ever cure little boys of buying lace valentines for pretty little girls," he wrote in his essay on Whitman (4). This statement is one side of a blindness to reality that leads to his paranoid fulminations, on the last day of his life, against his wife. About Lindsay's relationships with women, Masters tells us,

> He would have been happier as a celibate; but after forty he could not stand the loneliness. . . . Elizabeth Conner made him a wife as much adapted to his needs as he could have found in the world . . . but he was a man whom religion did not suffice, and whom love and marriage left thirsty for the music that is divine. (356–57)

He died raging that she was a "tyrant-mother and scarlet woman who had taken his virginity" (360–61).

David Perkins, whose *History of Modern Poetry* is a good barometer of the standard thinking on such subjects, calls the line of development of American poetry that includes Lindsay—and Amy Lowell, Edgar Lee Masters, Carl Sandburg, Lola Ridge, Sara Teasdale, Ridgeley Torrence, Adelaide Crapsey, Edna St. Vincent Millay, Elinor Wylie, Robert Hillyer, Paul Lawrence Dunbar, Claude McKay, Jean Toomer, Countee Cullen, Langston Hughes, Stephen and William Benét, and many others—Popular Modernism, to differentiate it from the High Modernism of Eliot, Pound, Stevens, Williams, Moore, and others. The term is as good a euphemism for The Scrapheap as any—otherwise, it is difficult to see what Elinor Wylie, for instance, has in common with Countee Cullen and Vachel Lindsay, or in what way all these poets can be described as popular. Of this particular group, of course, several have been rehabilitated, particularly Hughes and Toomer; the resurrection of Edna St. Vincent Millay is under way even as I write. But for the most part, these writers increasingly are dead foot soldiers, burnt-out tanks, from the army Amy Lowell generaled for a time—insistently, loudly, and yet lovingly—through the course of one of the bloodiest poetry wars the world has ever known. In 1917 Lowell wrote:

> It is impossible for any one writing to-day not to be affected by the war. It has overwhelmed us like a tidal wave. It is the equinoctial storm which bounds a period. . . . [T]he war and the subject of this volume are not so far apart as might at first appear. . . . The welding together of the whole country which the war has brought about, the mobilizing of our whole population into a single, strenuous endeavour, has produced a more poignant sense of nationality than has recently been the case in this country of enormous spaces and heterogeneous population. . . . Long before the shadow of battle flung itself over the world, the travail of this idealism began. Slowly, painfully, it took on a shape, hidden away in the dreams and desires of unknown men. (*Tendencies* v, vi)

For Lowell as much as for Lindsay and Whitman—though her crusade, lacking any quasi-religious dimension, was intended to redeem the American idea of Beauty—the battle for the character of poetry was a battle for America's soul. "The impact of the new poetry was explosive," Heymann says, "and Amy set off a lot of the dynamite" (238).

David Perkins says of Lowell that

> what contributed more [than her poems] were her energy, shrewdness, determination, and pluck. By these virtues she thrust herself into prominence among the poets of her time, but her position was precarious. Her poetry, though often written with sensitivity and intelligence, could not justify the importance that seemed to be hers—that was hers if we think only of her leadership in promoting

the new art. . . . Miss Lowell, like Sandburg, H.D., Aldington, and
many other "new" poets, was "modern" only in some aspects of
form and style. In sensibility and imagination she was safely within
the fold of familiar Romantic tradition. (343, 344–45)

Stated another way, the problem with these poets is that they do not
fit with sufficient incisiveness into the modernist myth of discontinuity—they were new, but they were not new enough. This argument is an effective one—as long as one accepts the modernist
myth and does not look too closely at the "minor" poems of the likes
of Ezra Pound, or think of *The Cantos* as a process document in the
grand Romantic tradition that runs at least from Wordsworth and
Byron through Whitman, or consider that the line running unex-
pectedly from Emerson to the "minor" and conservative poet John
Crowe Ransom and thence to Robert Lowell and Sylvia Plath is one
of the most prominent strains of postmodern American poetry.

"The other modernism" is nothing more or less than a disrepu-
table zone of the junkyard we call the university library, where the
literary remains of an army of poets who lived and wrote and loved
and labored and stabbed one another in the back in the first quarter
of the twentieth century have been swept under—for better or
worse. The process whereby some writing comes to be valued in a
relatively permanent way and other writing disappears is not only
inevitable, it is part of the act of imagination whereby a culture inscribes its character on itself—a process whereby the body politic
writes its own large poem out of all the bits and pieces that the poems of even the "greatest" poets inevitably are. This creative act is
extraordinarily difficult to describe because, like Melville's whale, it
is so large that it cannot be seen; it is also cultural, not sacred—political, not mystical. The imagination is a splendid and dangerous
force, as responsible for the Battle of the Marne as for *Ulysses*.

If it is self-serving and short-sighted to assert, as many critics and
academics do, the unimpeachable authority of the Great Books list,
it is also sentimental to lament too much the fading of so much
writing that few have the time, courage, capacity, or desire to read.

What is necessary—at least to the enterprise of literary history—is to try to understand the living reality of the museum we inevitably tend to make of our "best" writing. The first principle of this reality is that the life of writing is never interested in the museum, however obsessed individual poets may sometimes be. For poets as poets, the tradition is not a beautiful arrangement of immutable Masterworks; it is a junkyard where every writer goes to steal parts. This process is utterly pragmatic and democratic insofar as, at any given moment, Vachel Lindsay or Amy Lowell may be as useful a source of poetic gears and pulleys as Pound or Eliot—even more useful, perhaps, because they are relatively unexpected sources. Poets who are dismissed from the museum inevitably go on serving in the junkyard, and sometimes secret allegiances become strikingly visible. The spare parts Allen Ginsberg stole from the rusty engine that is Lindsay, and which Lindsay stole from Blake before him, are quite plain. "I write poetry," Ginsberg recently wrote, "because my father reciting Shelly English poet & Vachel Lindsay American poet out loud gave example—big wind inspiration breath" (*Cosmopolitan Greetings* xiv). The "spontaneous bop prosody" of Jack Kerouac, Ginsberg, and the Beats—their "primitive" Roaring Boy antiliterature of jazz, Benzedrine, and neon signs—is a 1950s version of the Higher Vaudeville, and *On the Road* is the grand-nephew of Lindsay's "on the road" books, *A Handy Guide for Beggars and Adventures While Preaching the Gospel of Beauty*. The splendid tragi-bathetic psycho-vaudeville of John Berryman's *Dream Songs* likewise owes a major debt to Lindsay.

Any poetry of genuinely startling character, of originality and force, can define itself only against a background of work that is busy exhausting material of less originality and force. Someone must define the average; someone must foreground the "poetic." There is as much necessity for literary history to understand this part of the cultural process as there is for it to understand what it defines as "greatness." For instance, much of Amy Lowell's mature writing reads, from our perspective, like the work of a rank workshop beginner.

I cannot see your face.

When I think of you,

It is your hands which I see.

Your hands

Sewing,

Holding a book,

Resting for a moment on the sill of a window.

My eyes keep always the sight of your hands,

But my heart holds the sound of your voice,

And the soft brightness which is your soul.

(*Pictures* 87)

The first seven lines of this are all right, one might say, though flat, prosaic, lacking in energy; the eighth seems as if it might be the beginning of a mistake; and the last two are simply awful. This is not one of Lowell's "good" poems, but its pattern is typical of her short lyrics: establish a picture in relatively clear and straightforward language, and then swerve into the (hopefully appropriately) emotional. This is part of the method of imagism, and if Pound tired of it quickly, it is obvious why: any method that so transparently lapses into a convention—as this one did in its own time—is readily exhausted. And yet in its time, against a backdrop of Georgian moral verse, this method was radical and energizing. It is modernist. And it gave rise to better things:

Well, John Keats,

I know how you felt when you swung out of the inn

And started up Box Hill after the moon.

Lord! How she twinkled in and out of the box bushes

Where they arched over the path.

How she peeked at you and tempted you,

And how you longed for the "naked waist" of her

You had put into your second canto.

You felt her silver running all over you.

(*Pictures* 253)

Vachel Lindsay's poems withstand this kind of textual scrutiny
even less well than Amy Lowell's. Lindsay himself would protest
that they were not written to withstand it. R.S.B. states Lindsay's
aesthetic well: "The explicitly poetical stage directions which accom-
pany these poems 'to be read aloud or chanted' initiate the reader at
once into [Lindsay's] art, and rather spoil him for the tame business
of reading." Unfortunately for Lindsay, history has, at least for our
time, made "the tame business of reading" the final arbiter of poetry; as the poet Marvin Bell once quipped, "If poetry is nothing but
music, what chance does it have against the real thing?" But this issue was far from settled in 1910, and it was part of the poetry war we
call modernism to settle it. The work of William Morrison Patterson
is one avenue of that settlement; science might have something to
say, for the modernists, about the hard and fast distinctions among
poetry, prose, and music as distinct facets of human rhythmical expression. But the epic forays and the impassioned performances of
Vachel Lindsay are another, and equally important, avenue. Like a
rock star, like a charismatic politician, he inflamed audiences; and it
is only with the luxury of hindsight that we can pretend to say with
certainty, as Amy Lowell said in jest, "Perhaps, after all, his failure is
merited."

Lowell, in fact, was certain that Lindsay's place was secure. As
she wrote breezily to her friend the poet Florence Ayscough in
1922:

> Ah, my dear, you are an innocent lamb! You have no idea of the
> rings of intrigue in this poetry business. The more successful I am,
> the more I am hated. . . . The public is more and more for me, the
> poets—that is, those less successful than I—more and more against
> me. I meet with no jealousy from men who have arrived, like Frost,
> Lindsay, and Sandburg, but I meet with nothing else from those of
> the lower rank. Meanwhile my books increase their sales, and I had
> twenty-five hundred people to hear me speak at Ann Arbor. (Damon
> 604)

Always paradoxical, even contradictory, Amy Lowell is herself very difficult to summarize. Vachel Lindsay, perhaps, came as close as anyone:

> given her aura and personality and her descent from a line of
> public-spirited lawyers and wealthy men of affairs, it sometimes
> seems a pity, [Lindsay] remarked, that she was so determined to
> become a poet. She would have been happier as the Senator from
> Massachusetts. (Heymann 279)

Lindsay, the William Jennings Bryan of poetry, might as well have been talking about himself. Less tough than Lowell, less singular of will, and far less wealthy, by the late 1920s Vachel Lindsay could already feel himself sliding into the junkyard. The book he thought his greatest achievement—the visionary prose work *Golden Book of Springfield*, which is his *Jerusalem* and which he labored over for years—vanished virtually without comment. And at that moment a poet who had cast himself as a literatus from the beginning suddenly realized he had turned into nothing but a littérateur. In 1908 and 1909, Lindsay had stood on the streets of Springfield handing out his socialist-mystical "War Bulletins" to anyone who would take one, declaiming to his fellow Illinoisians,

> I have spent a great part of my few years fighting a soul battle for
> absolute liberty, for freedom from obligation, ease of conscience;
> independent from commercialism. I think I am farther from slavery
> than most men. But I have not complete freedom of speech. In my
> daily round of work I find myself taking counsel to please the stu-
> pid, the bigoted, the conservative, the impatient, the cheap. A good
> part of the time I can please these people, having a great deal in
> common with all of them.—but—
>
> *The things that go into the War Bulletin please me only. To the Devil
> with you, average reader. To Gehenna with your stupidity, your bigotry,
> your conservatism, your cheapness and your impatience!*
>
> *In each new Bulletin the war shall go faster and further. War! War!
> War!* (Prose 85)

This same man, years later, would say in print ("Adventures Preaching Hieroglyphic Sermons" xiii) that having "The Rose and the Lotus" printed for Congress was "the nearest that my life has ever come to politics."

By 1925 Lindsay found himself at the mercy of his own enormous "loving" audiences—and of trade publishing, to the blandishments of which he had gradually become addicted. America got him in the end—capitalism, crass careerism, and an almost childlike desire to please. But he was played false as much by his own lack of conviction about the substance of his visionary mission as by anything else. When the people of Springfield did not respond at once to the message of his "War Bulletins," like a Reagan-era politician he simply changed the message. Eleanor Ruggles says,

> [W]hat his extravagant language provoked from most who read it
> was a wave of mockery and from others a permanent distrust. . . .
> Even "the friends of my heart gave scorn," he wrote in his diary. . . .
> When he could write calmly on the subject, he declared that at
> the time he had gone no farther on that path. "I see no particular
> benefit in going down an alley of swords. Whenever I see Hate in
> the way, I go no farther." (Ruggles 148)

Lindsay had invented his "Higher Vaudeville" style precisely in order "to compel attention."

> Lindsay was weary of having his early, delicately imaginative poems
> ignored. It occurred to him that his friends, or many of them, considered *General Booth* his best poem simply because the bold
> rhythm and trick devices—instructions in the margin and naming
> of a tune—*forced* their notice.
>
> In the same way, when he bawled the *Kallyope* or parts of the
> unfinished *Congo* at them, though they mostly overlooked the message, they were terrifically excited by the "Whoops" and the "Boom-lays" and they swore to him these new poems were fine and much
> easier on the understanding than the little filigree pieces, moon
> verses and the like, that he used to bring around. (Ruggles 211)

But even by the early 1920s, having performed poems in this same style repeatedly—indeed having repeatedly performed the same handful of poems—Lindsay had to admit that he himself disliked them. In December 1922 he wrote to Harriet Moody:

> I utterly dislike reciting. My audiences demand just two pieces that I utterly abhor: Booth and the Congo. They will *pay to hear them* any time—and then the sooner I leave town the better; as far as the bulk of the audience is concerned. And they will not buy one book, unless *urged*. . . . The whole jazzy notion of my work is based on the eagerness of my first year of reciting after I had faced contempt for so long. But it is as hard to endure as contempt, and has nothing whatever to do with my ambitions and aspirations. . . . [A]llow me, my good friend and noble hearted Cordelia—to be the Don Ivan, the Aztec, the Toltec, the Matador, not the jazzer, not the saxophone. (*Letters* 259, 260, 261)

And a month later, he wrote to friends,

> [T]hough people call me a "poet" they have not the least notion that an imagination burnt out by too much reiteration is worse than physical sickness. People howl for me to recite Booth and the Congo till I am ready to vomit. And they threaten me if I refuse, till I am ready to swear myself crazy. . . . The whole world is in a conspiracy to sell for a high price my stalest fancies and to kill off all my new ones. (*Letters* 267–68)

The terrible irony—which Lindsay came to understand perfectly— is that he did not believe in the "modern" qualities of the work that made him famous. He would much rather have lived in Poe's "Ulalume" than in any reality he knew. Of the poetry of the Higher Vaudeville, he wrote,

> One composes it not by listening to the inner voice and following the gleam—but by pounding the table with a ruler and looking out the window at the electric signs. Also by going to vaudeville, which I

have all my life abhorred. I at last grasp what those painted folks are up to. (Ruggles 211)

Like American culture generally in the 1920s, 1930s, and 1940s, Lindsay was willing and able both to exploit and to disparage African American music, which he found simultaneously powerful and frightening—jazz, blues, and the white imitation thereof that was vaudeville. "Why do I curse the jazz of this hotel?" he wrote in 1924; "I like the slower tom-toms of the sea" (*Poems* 576). And his poem "A Curse for the Saxophone," written in the same year, associates the instrument and its characteristic music with Cain and all human evil since:

> Give me a city where they play the silver flute. . .
> Where the xylophone and saxophone and radio are mute. . . .
> What did Judas do with his silver thirty pieces?
> Bought himself a saxophone and played "The Beale Street Blues." . . .
> None but an assassin would enjoy this horn.

> (*Poems* 577–78)

Lindsay desired purity, a poetry of the inner voice and the "gleam," not poetry of the saxophone; but he was compelled by his relationship with his audience toward the impure "jazz" poetry of the ruler on the table. Attempting to pursue both at once, he pressed the myth of the visionary poet surrounded by the leaden artifacts of a fallen world so far and so hard, made of it such a ritual of the "poetic," that no one would take up that mantle again for a quarter century.

It was the poetry of the saxophone that made his audiences give him the love he so desired—and it was the saxophone and the electric signs out the window that were to prevail in the poetry of the future. In 1925, at the end of his inscription to Langston Hughes on the flyleaf of Lowell's biography of Keats, Lindsay wrote,

> Do not let any lionizers stampede you. Hide and write and study and think. I know what factions do. Beware of them. I know what

flatterers do. Beware of them. I know what lionizers do. Beware of them. Good wishes to you indeed. (*Letters* 364)

But like so many of us, Lindsay failed to take his own advice. He knew that poetry is relatedness but failed to understand the subtlety and the extraordinary power of that dimension of his vocation, what Woolf called the "difficult business of intimacy." She knew, as Lindsay did not, the challenge and the danger of that imperative. Lindsay wanted Inspiration, but all he was granted was the world.

As Cary Nelson puts it, "it is partly [Lindsay's] failure to achieve his impossible ambitions—ambitions extracted from ideals circulating in the culture at large—that is his gift to future generations" (69). If the character of a poet—like the character of a poem, of a nation, of what is human—is at once an inscribed and inscribing thing, then from the spectacular tragicomic collapse of a Vachel Lindsay, we can learn volumes about the eternal pain of *kharakter*, the zone where the excruciating tip of the inscribing tool touches the blank page of the book that, as Whitman insists, is no book at all but is selfhood. And we can learn from a writer such as Lindsay, too, the inevitable and bitter cost of pitting human character—which individually and collectively we create, and which, in December of any year you choose, can suddenly change—against the sheer granite of human nature. Lindsay learned this lesson early on, and to his grief promptly forgot it, as he reveals in the closing stanza of his awkward, moving little poem "Why I Voted the Socialist Ticket," written before the Higher Vaudeville, the various seductions of mass audience, his defeat at the hands of his own new convention, and his final madness:

> Come let us vote against our human nature,
> Crying to God in all the polling places
> To heal our everlasting sinfulness
> And make us sages with transfigured faces.

"Sen-Sen," Censorship, Obscenity, Secrecy

Slapping the Face of the Body Politic

> I'm talking about power, and I'm talking about you.
>
> —Ewing Campbell, "Sister Love"

In January 1990, when I was editing *New England Review*, a Texas writer named Ewing Campbell (*Weave It like Nightfall; The Rincón Triptych; Piranesi's Dream*) received a National Endowment for the Arts fellowship in the field of creative writing/fiction. There was, I imagine, appropriate celebration in Hearne, where Campbell then lived. An NEA fellowship is both an honor and a very useful professional dispensation; Campbell was able almost immediately to take time off from his job in the English Department at Texas A&M to devote his full attention to writing. This, of course, is precisely what NEA fellowships are supposed to be for; and as Campbell is a proven writer and a disciplined craftsman, the investment of tax dollars in his work would appear to have more chance than most of bearing fruit.

However, it was not long before circumstances conspired to cloud Campbell's pleasure in his prospects and to divert his attention from writing. Reading the *AWP Chronicle* in February, he discovered what we now all know: that "In November, AWP [Associated Writing Programs] learned that the National Endowment for the Arts had flagged 5 creative writing fellowships as 'questionable' in light of the new appropriation bill that forbids the use of federal monies for funding obscene works" ("New Coalition" 20). The March/April issue of the *Chronicle* amplifies the issue:

> Stephen Goodwin, then director of the NEA's Literature Program, flagged five individual fellowship applications as questionable in light of the appropriation bill which forbids funding of projects that "may be considered obscene, including but not limited to, depictions of sadomasochism, homoeroticism, the sexual exploitation of children, or individuals engaged in sex acts and which, when taken as a whole, do not have serious literary, artistic, political, or scientific value." Although the NEA's panel of peer review had recommended that those five applicants receive fellowships, Goodwin brought the applications to the attention of [NEA chair John] Frohnmayer, who took the five applications before the National Council on the Arts, which is the Presidentially appointed body that oversees the NEA. The council upheld the NEA panel's decision to award the fellowships. (16)

In spite of this intervention, Campbell's fellowship was awarded —and he had received the funds by the time he became aware of these developments at the NEA. All's well that ends well, some might be inclined to say. But the issue of public funding for the arts was heating up rapidly by late February, and Campbell was uneasy on many counts. Because he thinks of himself as a transgressive writer, Campbell realized it was possible that his might have been one of the five "flagged" applications. "Any one of the applications for fiction fellowships could have been investigated," he told me in a telephone conversation on June 2. "Purely from a statistical vantage point, there was a chance mine was one of the five. And when I looked at the topics cited in the congressional language, I realized I could have been suspect on every count."

For a while, Campbell vacillated. When the now-infamous March 6 letter from North Carolina senator Jesse Helms to comptroller general Charles Bowsher became public—the letter that begins "(First of all, because of the nature of the enclosed material, I urge that great care be taken to assure that your women associates not be exposed to the material)"—Campbell learned the names of three of what we'll call The NEA Five: three women writers whose work was flagged because of lesbian subject matter. That left only two unidentified, cutting the odds considerably. Still, Campbell was suspicious. On the one hand, there was a certain healthy self-interest involved; on the other, larger issues were at stake.

A telephone call to the National Endowment yielded nothing. Campbell was told that the whole matter had been "blown out of proportion"; but when he asked point-blank whether he could find out whether his was one of the five flagged applications, he was informed in no uncertain terms that no facts about the procedure would be forthcoming from the NEA. That information was not available to the public.

Meanwhile, Campbell received what he calls "a perfunctory letter" from Texas congressman Joe Barton congratulating him for receiving an NEA fellowship. "At some point it occurred to me," Campbell says, "that perhaps Barton could obtain the information I wanted. So I called his office and talked to a secretary, who informed me that in order to find out anything, I would have to sign a form waiving my right to privacy."

In due course the form arrived, and on March 25 Campbell completed it and sent it back to Representative Barton's office. The form—a copy of the completed version of which Campbell sent to me—is a simple enough one-pager; at the top it says, "I hereby authorize Congressman Joe Barton to request on my behalf, pertinent to the Freedom of Information and Privacy Act, access to informa-

tion concerning me in the files of," and there follows a blank in
which the words "National Endowment for the Arts—Literature Program" have been typed. Then, after the usual blanks for name, address, social security number, and the like, there are two questions,
with blanks for answers. Campbell's form—questions and answers—reads as follows:

BRIEFLY, STATE THE OUTCOME YOU ARE SEEKING

Given the problem stated below, I want to know if I was one of the
five writers singled out by the NEA for a special review. If I was not
one of that number, I would like to be assured of that fact.

PLEASE STATE THE NATURE OF YOUR PROBLEM (BE SPECIFIC):

After all recipients of the 1990 NEA literary fellowship grants had
been recommended, NEA Chairman John Frohnmayer asked for a
special review of work by five writers that the NEA thought might
raise problems in light of new legislation. It would be helpful to me
as a writer who might have been "questioned" to know if my work
borders on what might be considered obscene.

In late May, Campbell got his answer. Representative Barton's
office forwarded to him a letter written to Barton by Frohnmayer,
dated May 14. The letter runs to nearly two pages; it deserves to be
quoted at length. After outlining the situation more or less as I have
described it above, Frohnmayer gets down to brass tacks. The pertinent passages are these:

I requested Council discussion in light of the recent FY 90 appropriations language prohibiting the funding of work, when taken as a
whole, which could be considered obscene and lacking serious
literary, artistic, political or scientific value. Mr. Campbell's manuscript was one of the five reviewed, but neither Mr. Campbell, nor
any of the other writers was referred to individually. The discussion
was broad in nature and focused more on the problem of imple-
menting the congressional language than on the specifics of the

manuscripts themselves. None of the writers was named during the course of the Council's discussion. And, as you may know, these five writers were awarded fellowships.

In accordance with the Freedom of Information Act (FOIA), it is the Endowment's long standing policy not to release transcripts of closed portions of discussions by the National Council on the Arts to the public in order to preserve the free flow of information among Council members. Similarly, such panel materials are likewise protected. We withhold this information under exemption (b) (5) of the FOIA, as it is considered to be part of the deliberative process. We do, however, provide upon request, summaries of such information. With respect to your request, the Justice Department's guidance under FOIA provides that your request should be treated as a request from the general public because you do not serve on a committee or subcommittee which oversees the Endowment. However, in an effort to be as responsive as possible to your inquiry and to assure you that Mr. Campbell was not individually singled out during any part of the review by the Council, I have enclosed a report on the portion of the meeting of the National Council on the Arts which includes the discussion of the five manuscripts. Please understand that this report must be kept in confidence. (1–2)

So now Campbell knew that he was indeed one of The NEA Five. However, that was about all he knew. Frohnmayer does make clear that "neither Mr. Campbell, nor any of the other writers was referred to individually"; he also makes it sound as if even the manuscripts were hardly talked about—though the second paragraph does refer to "the discussion of the five manuscripts." Presumably Barton received the "report" to which Frohnmayer refers; but in keeping with Frohnmayer's request, Barton did not send a copy to Campbell. What was said by whom, and why—why Campbell's application was flagged in the first place—all that information was still not available to the public or to Ewing Campbell.

Enter *New England Review*. On receiving Frohnmayer's letter via

Barton, Campbell got in touch with me. *NER*, it turns out, is implicated in this matter, and I am personally implicated as well. In the
spring of 1988, when I was serving *NER* (then called *New England
Review and Bread Loaf Quarterly* or, more familiarly, *NER/BLQ*) as
guest editor—taking the place of then senior editor Sydney Lea, who
was on leave—I accepted a story of Campbell's, "Sister Love," and it
appeared in the Autumn 1988 issue. The relevance to the matter at
hand is simple: Campbell's application for a National Endowment
Fellowship in Creative Writing/Fiction included two sample short
stories, presented under the joint title "Sermons"; "Sister Love" was
one of them. Implicit in the decision to flag Campbell's fellowship
application, then, is the suggestion that *NER* has published writing
that Goodwin thought some monitor of the NEA might consider
"obscene" and lacking "literary, artistic, political, or scientific value."
These are serious imputations, *even though* the fellowship was
nevertheless forthcoming: serious for Campbell, in obvious ways;
serious for *New England Review* in ways that are a little less obvious
but nonetheless very real.

As I write, I am surrounded by piles of documents, mostly copies
of newspaper clippings (news stories, editorials, and the like—
many supplied by the Coalition of Writers' Organizations, acting as
an effective watchdog over these proceedings) published within the
past few months addressing the challenge facing the National Endowment for the Arts particularly and the controversies over public
funding for the arts and censorship generally. I say "controversies"
in the plural consciously and advisedly. Not only has this situation
generated a cyclone of newsprint, it has provided an effective focus
for a multitude of arguments. Anyone reading through this mass of
material is bound to feel bewilderment and a certain despair. Obviously, the matter strikes not simply a nerve, but a major ganglion;
partisans on both sides of the issue often seem less to be thinking
than twitching, like frogs' legs in a skillet.

One fact that strikes me even more forcibly than others is how
narrow many of the arguments are—how many focus on local mat-

ters of special interest, and thereby consciously or unconsciously skew the issues that seem to be at the heart of the matter. It is natural that it should be so, since everyone who is concerned about this problem at all is concerned in one way or another with local particulars, and those particulars are very important. Whether you are a member of the Moral Majority outraged over the public display of certain words or images "paid for" by taxpayers' dollars or an artist or director of an arts organization concerned about the availability of grants, what is happening within your own field of vision counts a great deal. Yet the size and suddenness of this cultural tornado indicates that it is part of a much larger national complex.

One night in 1979, while I was living in the intermountain west, I turned on my car radio and heard one of that state's congressmen utter—vis-à-vis the issue of in vitro fertilization, an issue then much in the news—the following sentence: "We must not allow scientists to have ideas that interfere with our picture of the universe."

I was not surprised to discover such a sentiment coming out of the darkness in that place and at that time. I was, however, puzzled— as I have often been puzzled, all my life—to find such a statement made part of an argument purporting to be ultrapatriotic. It should not have to be said, my reasoning goes, that the United States is deeply dedicated to those principles of freedom of thought, and of expression of thought, guaranteed by the First Amendment. That, at least, is what I have always understood. Freedom is freedom, I take it; isn't it therefore tautological that repression of thought and expression is not consonant with freedom of thought and expression? Isn't it obvious that the end of the free and open play of ideas among scientists, for instance, is the death of science itself?

But the ramifications of the congressman's repressive sentiment go far beyond the concerns of science. One of the great ethical challenges of the American experiment is, as has often been said, to provide freedom even—or especially—for ideas particular individuals among us may hate.

By now, I tell myself, all this ought to go without saying. But we all know it does not, because the situation I am describing is so familiar as to be archetypal. Many who call themselves patriots would extinguish freedom in the name of freedom; there is nothing surprising about the spectacle. But, familiar or not, it certainly is puzzling. Within a mental and rhetorical horizon where even tautologies can come unraveled, and where millions of people can witness that unraveling without a single qualm or a moment's doubt, where is bedrock? Where is the certainty of that "picture of the universe" in which the western congressman so sincerely believed and for which he was willing to squelch freedom of thought?

Or am I simply worried about the collapse of my own "picture of the universe"?

There are those who would reply that applying this argument to the issue of public funding for the arts is misplaced, irrelevant, illogical. There is what superficially appears to be a very simple and clear reply: that a refusal or failure to use government funding for the arts does not constitute censorship, and does not interfere with anyone's right to free expression; that if American taxpayers don't like art, if they are offended by it, then they ought to withhold their tax dollars from supporting the arts. "A central function of art is to redefine frontiers by outraging the placid," William Safire concedes; "but one central right of the taxpayer is to withdraw his consent from being pushed out to the cutting edge of anything. Conflict is built in; never forget who is paying for that microphone." Kansas senator Nancy Landon Kassebaum states the same argument more succinctly, if less colorfully, in a May 16, 1990, letter to David Levi Strauss: "Artistic expression is protected by the laws of our nation and will continue to be. It does not follow, however, that federal subsidies of artistic expression can be granted on an unconditional basis."

What interests me is the gap in this argument—what happens before and after the "but" in Safire's reasoning, before and after the "it does not follow" in Kassebaum's. Logically, legally, morally, Safire and Kassebaum are both right. The government is under no obligation whatsoever to fund the arts. Furthermore, even if the NEA and all other agencies, public and private, that support artists and arts organizations should disappear the first thing Monday morning, artists and arts organizations would go on, art would continue. The survival of art is not the issue; the *obligation* of taxpayers to fund the arts is simply a nonissue.

The question is rather the obverse: What is the cost to the country if taxpayers, or their elected officials, decide not to fund the arts? Safire's "but" is not the only possible outcome of the clause that precedes it; one might as logically rewrite the sentence to conclude, "therefore, the world needs its artists to be strong and healthy and bold, and the American taxpayer, who has no *obligation* to do so, would be wise to invest in the arts for the sake of his or her own future well-being." And Kassebaum might as well end by saying, "Nevertheless, we should invest tax dollars in the arts conditionally—provided the conditions are ones of fairness and freedom, not ones of censoriousness and repression. Science is judged according to the conditions of science, and government happily pays part of the bill; art likewise should be judged according to the standards of art."

Let's not be deceived; no one is proposing to give back the sixty-five cents per year the average taxpayer spends on the NEA. Congress will simply put these funds to other uses: building stealth bombers, bailing out savings and loans institutions, etc. The track record of the Reagan-Bush years does not suggest that the money will go to help the hungry, the homeless, the ignorant, or the ill. Why should the same taxpayers who paid for the cutting-edge technology of the Hubble Telescope (which is certainly busy changing our picture of the universe) be denied the opportunity to participate in the "cutting edge" of art?

In the spring of 1989, exactly ten years after I heard the western congressman speak about "pictures of the universe" on my car radio, I was asked to take part in a symposium concerning the situation of novelist Salman Rushdie. The symposium's title, "Can the Imagination Be Censored?" was suggested to the panel's organizer by Rushdie's own call to "the intellectual community" in England and abroad to "stand up for freedom of the imagination, which is an issue much larger than my book or indeed my life" (Editorial 1).

I was not then, nor am I now, certain that the symposium's title was intended to say precisely what it said; perhaps a metonymy was intended, and we were supposed to speak about whether the *products* of the imagination can be censored. However, given Rushdie's suggestive challenge and the seriousness of his position, I took and continue to take the title of the symposium as a literal question that demanded a literal answer. Yes, I maintained, the imagination—the imagination itself, as opposed to its mere products, which are obviously vulnerable—can be censored. However, the imagination can and will be censored *only* by the power of the imagination itself.

In the western world, we have a high Romantic concept of the nature and role of what we are pleased to call "imagination." There is not enough space here to define that concept or trace the history of it—nor is there any need to do so, since we all know more or less what it is. It will suffice for me to remind us that the aesthetic imagination is not the only imagination, that the products of art are not the only products of imagination. Politics is as much imagined as literature and religion are imagined. Furthermore, not all products of imagination are by definition benevolent, as we sometimes pretend to believe. The imagination, in fact, is quite ruthless—as much rattlesnake as angel. In some of its incarnations, it will just as soon kill you as look at you.

Censorship amounts to violence committed by the imagination against the imagination. In these terms, death is the ultimate censorship, and that part of the Muslim world that would take Rushdie's life understands the matter precisely, and without hypocrisy, in this way. For the individual imagination, censorship's final

form is execution or assassination; at the cultural level, it is geno-
cide; and at the level of the species, it is apocalypse, which can only
be carried out, we are reasonably sure, by gods, physicists, generals,
or some other of the imagination's yet uncreated avatars.

Salman Rushdie's situation, obviously, is an unusual one: a
strange face-off between an individual in his single body and a
whole body politic (one to which, in this case all the more oddly, the
individual in question does not belong). Naturally, Rushdie in this
frame of reference is a victim, besieged by an opponent he is
helpless to overcome; he is also heroic, an underdog giant-killer. His
only hope is his very insignificance: like David, he can slip beneath
Goliath's defenses; or like a microbe, he can hide in the belly of the
beast. Either way, we in the West are tempted to romanticize his
situation—perhaps to everyone's grief—or else to say, as Patrick
Buchanan essentially did (Campbell "Ayatollahs"), that he's made
his own bed, let him lie in it.

But consider the standoff between Rushdie and the Iranian government in another frame. In the guise of pure imagination poised
against pure imagination, the opponents are equivalent, equal. And
it is on this level that the central drama of the censorship of imagination will play itself out.

Harold Bloom, in *Ruin the Sacred Truths*, lucidly discusses what
he calls "the unresolvable aesthetic issue of poetry and belief,"
venturing the opinion that

secularization is itself a literary process. The scandal is the stubborn
resistance of imaginative literature to the categories of sacred and
secular. If you wish, you can insist that all high literature is secular,
or, should you desire it so, that all strong poetry is sacred. What I find
incoherent is the judgment that some authentic literary art is more
sacred or more secular than some other. Poetry and belief wander
about, together and apart, in a cosmological emptiness marked by the
limits of truth and meaning. Somewhere between truth and meaning can be found piled up a terrible heap of descriptions of God. (4)

That incoherence, that irreducible issue, is precisely the heart of the problem—Rushdie's as well as that of The NEA Five. From a Western perspective, Rushdie is suffering as much from the nonseparation of critical theory and power as the nonseparation of church and state. And however much artists in our culture may lament a lack of immediate political importance, however much we may long Romantically for the poet-king, we ought to recognize that in the will to assassinate Salman Rushdie we are witnessing precisely that: the visionary imagination with full political mandate and, within the bounds of its own poem, its body politic, no checks and balances. Either that, or—if we agree with Bloom that it is incoherent to separate sacred and secular in the realm of texts—we must admit that Rushdie is as much or as little a prophet as any of the poets of Islam or Christianity or any other religion. And in that case, the struggle is fully—and, bizarre to say, quite literally—a Blakean standoff of the Enumerations versus the Emanations.

Meanwhile, Salman Rushdie must live underground in order to preserve his life; the majority of us can only dimly imagine the personal toll such measures must exact. "It's his Word against mine," says Rushdie's namesake, the character Salman, trickster-scribe to the prophet Mahound in The Satanic Verses (368), and Rushdie has lived to see his bad pun turn into a jeremiad.

The Rushdie affair plunged us all, like it or not, into incoherent territory, Bloom's cosmological emptiness, and I can foresee no clear or fortunate way out. If all one's political and moral instincts tell one (as mine tell me) that surely no book ever written, not the Bible or the Koran and certainly not The Satanic Verses, is worth killing for, Rushdie's situation reveals that this "truth" is not self-evident to political or religious leaders who are convinced of the ascendancy of their various Truths or "pictures of the universe"—any more than it is self-evident to all artists, who are sometimes convinced of the ascendancy of their own meanings. (I take as evidence Faulkner's notorious comment, "If a writer has to rob his mother, he will not hesitate; the 'Ode on a Grecian Urn' is worth any number of old ladies" [Blotner 1594].)

"Political and moral instincts," therefore, cannot be simply trusted but must be criticized without ceasing, examined and tested, revised if found wanting, abandoned if found inadequate, upheld only if proved fruitful; advocates of different pictures of the universe must learn to argue with passion but without violence. However familiar this sort of rhetoric may seem to citizens of the United States, such practice must logically lead to a radical agnosticism that would consider politics, religion, philosophy, science, literary theory, and even art (which we most often think of as a *creature* of the imagination) to be aspects of a central effort aimed at effectively criticizing the various forms the imagination produces, lest we become their slaves. No society of which I know has come close to embodying such a position. Certainly ours has not.

In a *New York Review of Books* critique of Rita Felski's *Beyond Feminist Aesthetics: Feminist Literature and Social Change*, Helen Vendler writes,

[Felski] is ambivalent about what has come to be called "the autonomy of the work of art"—that is, its independence of any social ideology, its aims beyond the limited one of representation. She repeats the old accusation—that emphasis on the autonomy of the work of art "has helped to encourage a mystification of art as a quasi-transcendental sphere . . .perpetuating the myth of the great artist as solitary genius." Does she mean that there are no great artists? Or that they were not geniuses? Or that they were great geniuses but not solitary? Or what? Simply to say that Beethoven came out of the German musical tradition and was supported by patrons . . . does not mean that he was not also a great artist and a solitary genius. The absence of female Beethovens may perhaps be explained by the absence of instruction and patronage for women, but instruction and patronage alone do not explain why one instructed and supported artist turns out to be Beethoven and another does not.

The "myth of the great artist as solitary genius" has enough truth to it to survive. (20)

Well, yes. But the fact that a myth survives—even the fact that there is a certain truth to it—does not mean that it may not also be a mystification, an incoherence, a fetish. To put forth the essentially metaphysical proposition that Beethoven was a "solitary genius" does not explain why he, and not someone else, turned out to be Beethoven any more than do appeals to "instruction and patronage alone." Why must it be either/or? And (to state the painfully obvious) if "genius" falls, like mercy, as the rain from heaven, why does it not fall as often on women as on men, on African Americans and Native Americans as on whites, on the poor as on the middle class and the wealthy—unless there is a god of genius who is a rich old white man?

One effect of the current climate of acrimony about the cluster of issues that the question of public funding for the arts brings out into the open is this: Surely everyone now can see that artists are not "solitary," no matter how much time they spend alone. It is true a certain amount of (though by no means all) art is produced by individuals working in physical isolation. It is also true that art, as art, is communal insofar as it must initially imply, and ultimately connect with, an audience in order to *be* art at all (what would Emily Dickinson's poems be had no one ever discovered them, had they vanished forever?); and art is communal insofar as it arises inexorably out of traditions and cultural institutions. Salman Rushdie, Ewing Campbell, Emily Dickinson, Beethoven may labor away incessantly in the "solitude" of their hermetic workplaces; but the world is with them—and let the political climate alter in the right (or the wrong) way, and the world will batter down their doors, bearing, as the case may be, laurels or handcuffs. If you don't believe me, ask Václav Havel. Ask Irina Ratushinskaya. These writers have had it both ways.

What Vendler says is no truer than she says it is. Her passionate espousal of what her language reveals to be a half-truth (against what she implicitly admits that Felski "ambivalently" maintains to be no more than a counter-half-truth) arises out of the fact that she herself, as a theorist, has a vested interest in the myth. Vendler bases her mode of criticism—and hers is a criticism I often admire—on a Romantic glorification of sensibility, of the unique freestanding self as the sine qua non of art. It works, as theory, as far as it goes; and it goes far enough, most likely, to survive as theory. But such glorifications have a way of crumbling in the face of hard realities. Vendler's way of seeing would appear to put her—and I trust she would be horrified at the thought, but nevertheless—implicitly in league with Senator Helms and anyone else who would say to American artists, "Go off and do what you do in the privacy of your own homes, if you must do it; but don't expect American taxpayers to support your effort (and don't show what you write or paint or compose to our womenfolk). If you are solitary, go be solitary. How else can you be a genius, anyway?"

No matter how freestanding Rushdie may have felt as he composed *The Satanic Verses* (which I suspect was not very, given his canniness), no matter how freestanding Ewing Campbell may have felt as he wrote the two stories he submitted to the NEA, each understands now that he was not and is not living and thinking and working alone.

"Imagine the chilling effect," Campbell writes in a *Houston Chronicle* editorial, "of having a U.S. Senator take a personal, hostile interest in you." He continues,

> Most of us cannot imagine ourselves as important enough to warrant secret scrutiny at the highest levels of government. Each of us hopes our elected and appointed officials are dealing honestly and competently with important issues, not trivializing art or the business of democracy.
>
> That certainly was how I felt when I read that out of the 97 writers recommended for NEA creative-writing fellowships, five had their applications held up and subjected to a special review. I understood the implications of such a special review and intellectually deplored the action. But I did not feel it firsthand as an emotional reality. You see, it was still an abstract principle to me.

That is, until I received a letter in late May written by the endowment's chairman . . . documenting that "Mr. Campbell's manuscript
. . . was one of the five reviewed". . . . Suddenly the abstract principle
became concrete and particular.

Editors of literary quarterlies are always forcibly aware of contin-
gency. We live (and more often die) where art and the marketplace
part company. One way or another, virtually all literary quarterlies
are subsidized. Though all editors are critics insofar as we read and
make decisions about what we read, and though all editors are perforce theorists of one kind or another insofar as we are critics, we are
also pragmatists, creatures of *praxis*, part of the ebb and flow of
public moods. It is not that literary quarterlies require government
funding to survive—some do and some do not. It is, rather, that a
repressive or censorious atmosphere in government affects everyone in the culture. Quarterlies do not rely on commodity exchange
for bread and butter, paper and ink, but their existence depends on
the goodwill and tolerance of subscribers, donors, and subsidizers,
whether individuals or institutions, grant-giving foundations or
government agencies. Furthermore, editors are not exempt from
the effects of repressiveness; consciously or unconsciously, the ire of
Jesse Helms may make us uneasy about publishing transgressive
works, even if we are convinced that they possess high artistic merit.
Nothing is easier than for an editor to slip a story or poem back in its
return envelope with a rejection slip; how much more likely are editors to do so upon feeling the pressure of congresspeople or trustees
at their backs?

We all want to believe in our own courage; but the performance
of Goodwin and Frohnmayer in the matter of The NEA Five is a dis-
couraging example. Isn't it likely that the applications were flagged
because the administrators wanted to pass the buck to the National
Council—which, to its everlasting credit, awarded the fellowships
anyway? And editors are as prone to this kind of waffling as anyone.
We are even more prone, perhaps, because we have the illusion that
what we reject is more or less a private matter. Readers read what we

publish; only rejected writers know what we reject, and they don't necessarily know the reasons. But editors are no more solitary than artists. What we do belongs not to ourselves alone, but to the culture and to the world.

"[A] profound chilling effect," reads a document entitled "Artistic Freedom: Our American Heritage" issued by artists and arts organizations gathered in Washington at the behest of Montana congressman Pat Williams, a staunch supporter of public arts funding, "now afflicts the arts and the exchange between artists, arts organizations, audiences and their congressional representatives." One might as well add editors and publishers to this list. The trickle down from the big congressional chill dampens us all. This dampening *is* censorship of the imagination; it is intimidation; it is violence done by one "picture of the universe" to another. The forces of censoriousness are led by those who cannot bear to have their image of the world transgressed or even questioned by anyone, those who are not wise enough and tolerant enough to live up to the fundamental American injunction to ensure freedom of ideas, even ideas you yourself may hate.

This injunction is not a law of nature, by any means. It is an invention, a part of the social contract that is the United States as a body politic. It can be changed, certainly—and there are those who would change it, often in the name of ultraconservatism, in order to protect us against what they quite sincerely believe are "un-American" ideas, unwilling to admit that under the terms of the injunction, *no* idea is or can ever be "un-American"—by definition. The changes they would make, paradoxically, are not evolutionary and would not be undertaken to improve cultural conditions for us all; their changes would be retrograde, undertaken to initiate the end of democratic evolution, in the name of a monolithic and finally static picture of the universe: change in the name of the death of change. This is the fundamental borderline over which the current war is being fought.

The poet Robert Pinsky has written that artists have two responsibilities: to continue their art as tradition, and to transgress it:

[T]he idea of social responsibility seems to raise a powerful contradiction, in the light of another intuited principle, freedom. The poet
needs to feel utterly free, yet answerable. . . . "All poetry is political."
The act of judgment prior to the vision of any poem is a social judgment. It always embodies, I believe, a resistance or transformation
of communal values. . . . The poet's first social responsibility, to
continue the art, can be filled only through the second, opposed
responsibility to change the terms of the art as given—and it is
given socially, which is to say politically. What that will mean in the
next poem anyone writes is by definition unknowable, with all the
possibility of art. (85, 98–99)

Good art—as William Safire has so handily reminded us—is always
transgressive. That is not because artists are irresponsible children
(some artists may be, but good ones rarely are) as some would have
us believe, but because the world is terribly imperfect, as are human
institutions; the world, and institutions, must be challenged in
order to evolve. Art transgresses institutions in the name of beauty
and joy, too, because our institutions are so often ugly and dreary.
But art is also communal, upholding certain values even as it challenges them. It transgresses them to reveal their weaknesses, yes,
but also to demonstrate their strength. To deny art the right to do the
one is to deny it the power to do the other. Though art can survive
well enough without the NEA, the gutting of that organization is a
gesture of violent social denial of art's mission. Artists can survive
this disenfranchisement; but to deny taxpayers the opportunity to
fund the arts is to disenfranchise *them* from participation in a fundamental part of their, and their society's, process of life and
growth.

Why was Ewing Campbell's fiction flagged at the NEA?
    At the risk of sounding self-serving, I want to emphasize what a
splendid story Campbell's "Sister Love" is. I can do this with a fairly
clear conscience, since I'm not the only one who thinks so. The
story was enthusiastically received and unanimously accepted by

the entire staff at *New England Review/Bread Loaf Quarterly*; further-more, it was subsequently noticed by Charis W. Conn, associate editor of *Harper's*, who wrote to Campbell on February 8, 1989, "I was very impressed with your story, 'Sister Love,' in a recent issue of *NER/BLQ*. I wonder if you would consider submitting some of your work to me at Harper's? I would be pleased to see it." Later in 1989, "Sister Love" was reprinted in *New Growth: Contemporary Short Stories by Texas Writers* (San Antonio: Corona). In his introduction to that volume, editor Lyman Grant says, "Ewing Campbell recreates the voice of 'Sister Love,' coming to us over border radio, in a pitch-perfect rendition of a contemporary oral tradition" (x).

Reviews of *New Growth* have been enthusiastic about "Sister Love" as well. Bryce Milligan of the *San Antonio Light* calls it the "literary gem" of the collection, "a tour de force tour of the Joycean confessions of a border radio preacher (read 'priestess'), during which Sister Love recounts her conversion. We think" (15). Dave Oliphant writes in the *Texas Observer*, "Campbell carries the reader along on an apocalyptic ride from the Midwest through Arkansas and on to Alpine, where 'the gutters ran dark and iridescent with crickets as the bus pulled in'. . . . The story is sheer fun, both as touching satire and as prose fiction that uses language in an exciting and surprising fashion" (19).

Beautifully crafted, "Sister Love" is deeply aware of the literary traditions that it evokes and with which it wittily and tellingly plays. The story is spun out of the passage in *Ulysses* that occurs at the very end of the "Oxen of the Sun" chapter (a passage in which Joyce himself is being resolutely Shakespearean while simultaneously pretending to be American):

> Then outspake medical Dick to his comrade medical Davy. Chris-ticle, who's this excrement yellow gospeller on the Merrion hall?
> Elijah is coming! Washed in the blood of the Lamb. Come on you winefizzling, ginsizzling, booseguzzling existences! Come on, you dog-gone, bullnecked, beetlebrowed, hogjowled, peanutbrained, weaseleyed fourflushers, false alarms and excess baggage! Come on,

you triple extract of infamy! Alexander J Christ Dowie, that's my
name, that's yanked to glory most half this planet from Frisco beach
to Vladivostok. The Diety ain't no nickel dime bumshow. I put it to
you . . . He's the grandest thing yet and don't you forget it. Shout
salvation in King Jesus. You'll need to rise precious early, you sinner
there, if you want to diddle the Almighty God. Pflaaaap! Not half.
He's got a coughmixture with a punch in it for you, my friend, in
his back pocket. Just you try it on. (349)

Sister Love is Campbell's turn on Joyce's American evangelical
cough syrup flimflam man; she is a female preacher broadcasting
over supercharged radio airwaves from south of the Tex-Mex border:

Come on, you lumberjacks of the Northwest, you beer-guzzling, bar-
brawling sons of the mackinaw, come on, you vets of the Salmon
Wars. It's here you get the veterans' preference. No age discrimina-
tion if you enlist in love's struggle. Come on, you isolated and
afflicted Canucks, living in a cold country. You too, you backsliders
of the Bible Belt. You former football players, gamblers, junkies.
Come on to Sister Love, here at Station XERF, Cuidad [sic] Acuña,
Coahuila, Mexico, across the last frontier of the Rio Grande.
    I'm talking about power, and I'm talking about you. . . . This ain't
no lullaby song for the fainthearted; it's about someone sinking as
low as a human possibly can. (95)

The story goes on to detail—in precise satire of a typical Protestant
confessional style—that "sinking," and it revels in the scurrilous-
ness of the details. Campbell tells me that he began writing the story
working in the spirit of a jazz musician, picking up a theme from a
great exemplar and then riffing on it, modulating it, using it as a
basis for invention and discovery. If that's an apt metaphor, then it
seems to me that Campbell gets a great deal of mileage out of playing Joyce in the key of Voltaire. Sister Love, like Candide, sets out as
an innocent but is immediately, and quite literally, disabused by a
cynical, dangerous, and scatalogical world:

It's about family and no family, about love gone mad and lust and incest because as soon as my father, ladies and gentlemen—yes, my natural father—quit looking at Cissy and saw I was changing, my figure beginning to develop, he couldn't keep his eyes off me—or his hands. . . .

Where was a mother's love then, brothers and sisters? Instead of accusations and recriminations, where was that love? Berated, blamed, beaten, and driven from home, I was thrown into the hands of a druggist-turned-abortionist who said he could put things right. That was my birthright, damned with a face and a body men wanted. Some of you listening out there know what I'm talking about. Some of you would give all you have for such a bargain. Because you want passion; you want euphoria; you want to be loved. Come on. You know it's true; you want to be loved, and that's the deception. (95)

Incest, child abuse, abortion, drugs, sexual passion, scatology, venereal disease, abuse of authority, the linking of sexuality with religion—certainly this story is about all these things. But is it "obscene"?

First, examine the language. Profanity and the sexually graphic are often considered symptoms of "obscenity." The passages here cited are representative; "Sister Love" contains absolutely nothing that could be described as profanity, nothing that could be labeled sexually explicit—sexual acts are declared and alluded to but are hardly described. You could, if you wanted to, read this story at a meeting of the Missionary Society. No doubt the missionaries would be set back on their heels by it—but not on account of obscenity. What would disturb the missionaries would be the religious and political transgressiveness of the story. Inspired by the downfall of the likes of Jimmy Swaggert and Jim Bakker, and by the public display of cynically amnesiac falsifying that characterized the Irangate hearings, "Sister Love" is, as Oliphant says, "touching satire." The object of the satire is the peculiarly American Bible Belt fundamen-

talist version of Christianity, which Campbell depicts as a materialis-
tic, power-mongering nihilism taking relentless advantage of an innocent—an innocent who, once she has ceased to be innocent, is
intelligent enough to get back her own.

While "Sen-Sen," the second story submitted to the NEA as part
of Campbell's fellowship application, is stylistically very different
from "Sister Love"—a more conventional first-person narrative—its
thematic concerns are the same: A boy whose mother has undergone a conversion experience and become deeply moralistic and repressive meets another boy more or less his own age who is a child
evangelist, only to discover that the evangelist-boy is much farther
gone in "the ways of the world" than he is and is even more under
the thumb of a grasping mother and a collection-skimming Texas
preacher who has clearly pederastic designs on him. Like "Sister
Love," "Sen-Sen" is, as far as I can see, in no way obscene. Even if
either of these stories contained so-called explicitly sexual material
(which they do not) and even if they employed profanity (which they
do not), the artfulness of this material, its intelligence and splendid
craftsmanship, reveals that Campbell's fiction, taken as a whole or
in any of its parts, has obvious artistic merit.

What, then, is going on? How could such good writing—including fiction admired by a reputable literary magazine, various editors, anthologists, reviewers, *and* the jury of Campbell's literary
peers who constituted the NEA's literature panel—be flagged in the
ultimate stages of consideration at the NEA?

Part of the problem is that we cannot know the answers to these
questions. The NEA isn't saying; the National Council isn't saying.
Campbell can't discover the particular reasons for his work's being
flagged, and neither can any of the rest of us. (I hesitate even to
point out the painfully obvious Kafkaesque irony in this situation:
that in a country where every credit card company has access to personal information, a writer has to go through such a ceremony of
absurdity, communicating with an arts agency through a congressional middleman, only to be refused information about what has
been done with his work in that government agency.)

Certain conclusions, however, can be inferred.

Let me cite again *AWP Chronicle*'s description of "the appropriation bill which forbids funding of projects that 'may be considered obscene, including but not limited to, depictions of sadomasochism, homoeroticism, the sexual exploitation of children, or individuals engaged in sex acts and which, when taken as a whole, do not have serious literary, artistic, political, or scientific value.'" And let me refer again to Campbell's intuition that he "could have been suspect on every count." By this he means, I take it, that his stories do refer to sadomasochism, to homoeroticism, to the sexual exploitation of children, and to individuals engaged in sex acts. Naturally, the problem comes when various people begin to try to determine whether a work nevertheless has "serious literary value." And Campbell's instinct was to suspect that those who are the objects of his satire would be willfully obtuse when push came to shove.

A letter from Jesse Helms to Michael Chitwood, president of the North Carolina Writers Network, contains a revealing shift of emphasis in the issues involved:

> I would emphasize that my amendment "censors" nobody. It does *not* deprive any "artist" of his or her right of free expression. The amendment simply states that obscene *or blasphemous* art shall not be financed with federal funds. I submit that no artist, or anybody else, has an unqualified "right" to be subsidized by the taxpayers. (May 16, 1990; italics mine)

The legislation with which the NEA is having to contend does not say a word about religion, although the original bill did contain sanctions against "blasphemy." Committees softened the original proposal—and with good cause. Obscenity has forever been a vexed issue in the Congress and in the courts. Issues having to do with religious freedom and with separation of church and state are far less controversial, far more clear-cut. The legislation as passed was denatured to the point that Helms himself voted against it.

Once again, I state the obvious: obscenity and blasphemy are not the same thing. Campbell's stories could hardly be ruled obscene;

they could, however, be convicted of blasphemy in the star chamber of the god-king. (One wonders whether they might have escaped special notice had they not been jointly titled "Sermons"; perhaps instead he might have called them "Obscenities.")

Publicity makes clear what the wording of the legislation conceals: The obscenity issue is a mask for an essentially religiously based movement to limit basic American freedoms. What has happened in Ewing Campbell's case—in spite of the immediate outcome of the NEA's fellowship process—is a resonant gesture that is logically incoherent but politically clear. If work this good can fall under a shadow of suspicion—especially a shadow cast by people of essentially good will, such as Goodwin and Frohnmayer—then any good writer's work might soon be in trouble.

Helms, it appears, is a spokesman for those for whom Americanness is inseparable from Protestant Christianity. He and they are entitled to that opinion. Helms is not, however, entitled to mask one congressional agenda with another, illegitimate one. What he fears is that his "picture of the universe" is being contradicted by Campbell's fiction—or by any transgressive art. And it is. But if he is—as certainly he would tell you—a good and patriotic American citizen, he has a responsibility to uphold Campbell's right to contradict him. True, no artist has an "unqualified 'right' to be subsidized by the taxpayers." But no U.S. congressman has an unqualified right to legislate the moral universe—even if his constituency insists that he do so. No senator has the right to exercise incoherence and obfuscation so as to disenfranchise his constituency from participation in a vital cultural process. The argument must go on, and it must be loud and precise; it must be clear.

Salman Rushdie's situation should teach us how fortunate we are to live in a society in which presidents, high priests, assassins, and literary critics have separate offices and different job descriptions. What is needed is a means of making certain that the separation of these powers is upheld without producing a commensurate fragmentation of community in which politicians, tolerant adherents of various religions, artists, and the general public are hermetically partitioned. The basic form of the U.S. government, with its separation of powers under the aegis of a single system and its counterpoise of checks and balances, is an attempt at achieving such an ideal. If we can replicate that structure in the microcosm of the arts community, we'll all be better for it. In the best of all possible worlds, the rattlesnake can lie down with the angel. But if we give critics the power to cut off artists' hands by metaphysical fiat . . . well, you be the judge.

The NEA controversy, like the Rushdie affair, is a skirmish, an episode in an ancient and ongoing war that no one will ever win. As always, power is the presiding angel. But power is exactly what the imagination is all about. That's why we love it. That's why we must do all we can to foster its action among us (even surrender our precious tax dollars to it). That's also why we must not entirely trust it—in the hands of artists or priests or politicians or the Moral Majority or that amazing American fantasy creature, The Common Woman or Man. It can as easily turn to destruction as to creation, a fact that ought to be especially clear when it threatens—via censorship or any of the channels of force available to the aesthetic imagination, the political imagination, or any other you care to name—to negate those among its own creations that we find the most useful, the most benevolent, the most beautiful.

Middlebury, Vermont, 1990

Postscript

In the fifteen years that have transpired since I wrote this essay, the politics of censorship, arguments about public art, and tension between the religious and secular spheres of American culture have undergone many fascinating and troublesome mutations—so many that any effort at revising and "updating" the piece was doomed from the start, and so I have not attempted it. On the other hand, the core issues about the nature and role of the imagination are un-changed.

It is worth noting that the controversy about the National Endow-ment for the Arts has virtually vanished. The administration of George W. Bush, via the appointment of the neoformalist poet Dana Gioia as the Endowment's director, has found a legitimate way to make the activities of the organization palatable to the majority of its conservative base: simply by ensuring that the Endowment funds projects acceptable to that base. A characteristic story ("Fed Arts Funding: Naughty No More," April 22, 2005) in the *News and Advance* of Lynchburg, Virginia, reports,

> A decade after Congress threatened to kill it, the National En-dowment for the Arts is alive and well and looking squeaky clean.
>
> Gone are the controversies over federally sponsored homoerotic and crucifix-in-urine exhibits. "Do I want to bring out an offensive piece of art of no quality? Not on my watch," NEA Chairman Dana Gioia said in an interview. . . . Gioia's moves are winning rave re-views from some members of Congress who once voted to disband the NEA.
>
> "I wanted to abolish them," said Rep. Sue Myrick, R-N.C., now an NEA fan.

How one feels about this development will depend on how one feels about the category "squeaky clean." Personally, I have a grudging admiration for the simplicity of neoconservative strategy: The agency remains, government funding of public art goes on, the right is mostly happy, and the left has no traction. Gioia's statement is careful not to exclude the possibility that "offensive" art may be art of quality; the question "offensive to whom, and why?" does not come up. The threat of axing the NEA was deeply controversial; the co-opting of its core has been largely unproblematic. The smart-bomb cleverness of the move is typical of the new right; my guess is that it will next be applied to the Public Broadcasting Service, where the controversy is not about "obscenity" but ideology.

Meanwhile—on a front that is not merely related but identical—the so-called religious right has found strong new allies in the present government and seems determined to erode long-standing boundaries between church and state. New, and increasingly incisive, efforts attempt to place religiously inspired controls on the work of educators, scientists, and politicians; art scarcely enters the current debate except as a commodity that can be controlled with a V-chip (a role one might argue that Mr. Gioia is playing at the NEA). But my core argument about the nature of the imagination places artists alongside these others as participants in the ongoing evolution of humanity's "picture of the universe."

We face the same danger now that we faced in 1990 and likely in 990 as well, and will be facing in 9900 if we survive so long: that those who do not want humanity's picture of the universe to evolve will prevail. Fundamentalism of any order will insist that the truth is already known and that everyone had better knuckle under to it or, as Emerson succinctly puts it in "The Divinity School Address," "I will kill you." Americans find this attitude problematic when they encounter it, say, in an Islamic terrorist; would that not be sufficient reason not to want it practiced at home? Though the fatwa against Salman Rushdie seems to have lost its head of steam, the situation in which he found himself in the late 1980s has not vanished—rather, it is now everywhere.

To say that the events of September 11, 2001, changed everything has become commonplace. While the horrific importance of that day can hardly be overstated, it might be better to acknowledge that in terms of core issues, nothing was changed by it. An archetypal conflict has been given new energy, a new spin, a terrible amplification. Those who will kill you if you do not uphold their picture of the universe have new weapons to enforce their threats. As is so often the case when an "us" faces off against a "them," fundamentalists of this stripe are on both sides, and death remains the ultimate censorship.

Athens, Georgia, 2005

Inside the Avalanche

In the foreword of *The Fact of a Doorframe: Poems Selected and New, 1950–1984*, Adrienne Rich raises, with typical wisdom and incisiveness, a crucial issue about the relationship between craft and the particular consciousness of any poet:

> One task for the nineteen- or twenty-year-old poet who wrote the earliest poems here was to learn that she was neither unique nor universal, but a person in history. . . . The learning of poetic craft was much easier than knowing what to do with it—with the powers, temptations, privileges, potential deceptions, and two-edged weapons of language.

The complexities of this position—exemplified so fully in the body of Rich's work—I take as fundamental. Who writes my poems? Do they represent what I believe they represent, in either the aesthetic or the political meaning of *representation*?

A recent rereading of *Voyager*, John Unterecker's biography of Hart Crane, underscored for me the knot of unanswerable questions that must attend any meditation on biography and the art of poetry. How can one even begin to understand with any precision the connections between the details of Hart Crane's life—from the

most profound to the most mundane—and his poetry? Is it profit-
able to think, when we read *The Bridge*, of Crane's Cleveland adolescence, of his homosexuality, of his love of dancing, of his peculiar
autodidact's sense of literature and of the history of culture, of his
alcoholism, of his longing for visionary experience, of his father's
career as a manufacturer of luxury candies (he invented Life Savers
and sold the proletarian idea cheap), of his curious and dreary suicide? No, I want to say: The poetry is not informed by these particulars or any of a million others reported in Unterecker's massive
book, any more than our understanding of Crane's poems depends
on facts that have never and will never come to light. But at the same
time there obviously *is* a connection between every fact of Crane's
life—known or unknown—and his poems. Otherwise, there is no
reason for Crane's poems to have been written by Crane; they might
as well have been written by you or by me.

A poet thinks these thoughts with a certain desperation. How,
exactly, are the details of my life connected to the poems I write?
What does it mean to be "neither unique nor universal"? Why are
my poems, for better or worse, written by me and not by you or by
Hart Crane?

Poetry is no one thing; rather, as Foucault says of any genealogy,
poetry is "an unstable assemblage of faults, fissures, and heterogeneous layers that threaten the inheritor from within or underneath." In confronting any poet's body of work—in confronting poetry per se—it is as if we face a vast avalanche held back, perhaps, by
a system of cables and pulleys barely adequate to the task of imped-
ing its forward course even momentarily. Thinking of that agglom-
erate as a unity, we say to ourselves, "Look: there is *a cliff.*"

No matter how monolithic it may appear to any particular observer, poetry is constantly and forever in a state of dismemberment.
Therefore, the dismemberment of poetry is no source of concern
except as a condition to be described and studied—and admired.
The self, too, is an avalanche, not a unity, but it insists on experiencing its own collapse as a forward motion into the world, it insists on

describing itself *to* itself as *a* self. The only dismemberment that can matter—as a source of fear and exaltation—is the dismemberment of individual poets. This dismemberment matters because it is the only one that can lead to a resurrection. This is one of the reasons why the "tragic" life of such a poet as Hart Crane is of such interest to us; we imagine, arguably wrongly, that we see in it with particular clarity the torque and strain of living inside the avalanche.

There are good reasons for our preoccupation with such matters—even beyond the pleasures of gossip. For example, one of the most mysterious moments in the history of poetry, the genealogy of the art, is the moment when Walt Whitman became Walt Whitman: that is, from the point of view of criticism and biography, the moment when Whitman became the man capable of writing *Leaves of Grass*. The mistake is to conceive of such a thing as taking place all in a moment. The resurrection of Christ required three narrative days—and who knows how much time was required for Dionysus to pull himself together?

The world dismembers poets; only poetry dismembers poetry. (This will cease to be the case when the world elects to dismember humanity.)

Ohio Abstract: Hart Crane

Factory æther thickens over the milky lake at sunrise,
Imperially, like smoke from the last cigar of the Czar.
Bruised faces of stevedores clarify along the docks
As if a metaphysical fluoroscope were touching them

With infiltrating radiation—on the other side, the skeletal
Shape of a crane appears against white buildings.
The tannery whistle agitates. This is inescapably Cleveland.
It is morning now, and the bridge remains the bridge.

Down by the stockyard fence, a man in a pea-coat staggers.
He was up all night drinking dago red. A sailor let him
Suck his dick, then blackmailed him for ten dollars.
Now he'll work sixteen hours in a warehouse shifting

Crates of chocolate hearts stamped out for the glorious balls
Of a second-rate midwestern Gilded Age. It isn't the money
That worries him, the thirty cents an hour. It isn't top-hats
Or new puce gloves. He can't forget the synæsthesia,

The luminous foretaste of sweat, those syncopated mystical chimes
In the background of his fumbling at the fly-buttons,
The disciplined, improvised slant-rhyme of *denim* and *tongue*.
Blinding, the incense of horseshit in the gutter.

He chokes on the ecstatic rumble of the fourth dimension's
    junk-carts.
Lonely and stupid and sad, the *Don't you love me?* of the barges.
And what are those great water-birds writing down there by the
    garbage?
In this illusion of space, nothing could ever have existed.

Wrong sex. Wrong sense. Wrong city. Wrong bridge. Wrong life.
But who needs another elegy? No one ever dies here either.
It just goes on and on, gold foil on an assembly line, two tons
Of hearts for New York City. *Metaphor*, riffs the streetcar,

Is *bear over* in the literal Greek. But who says what
Or *how heavy*? Blackjack. Crowbar. Hammer. A man
Coldcocked by the shadow of a telephone pole. Think of all they
    tell you
The soul holds up in the men's room of the Tower of Light.

Maybe nothing ever meant more on earth than what it weighs.

"Ohio Abstract: Hart Crane" is not a poem based in any rigorous
way on the "facts" of the life of Hart Crane; neither is it autobiographical in any way I am able to recognize. Its genesis lies somewhere midway in my reading of Unterecker and of Crane's poems; it
also lies in my own struggle to discover the political and personal
consequences of beauty, both philosophically and as I have registered its irradiation through the untrustworthy Geiger counter of

my own flesh and nerves. Czeslaw Milosz's unsettling poem "*Ars Poetica?*" comes as close as anything I know to describing the ambiguous set of relations out of which such poems come:

> The purpose of poetry is to remind us
> how difficult it is to remain just one person,
> for our house is open, there are no keys in the doors,
> and invisible guests come in and out at will.

It is possible to regard the peculiar refraction connecting poetry and the details of a poet's life—as if they were two separate categories—as a productive synaesthesia. It is possible to describe the process that bears over the weight of history into the shape of a given poem as the highest form of metaphorical activity. It is possible to maintain, without being in the least mystical or psychologically reductive, that Crane's poems are not only Crane's poems, that mine or yours are not only mine or yours.

The world dismembers poets—but poetry, and poets, are part of the world. Unique? Universal? The white space between "ars" and "poetica" contains multitudes.

Ex Machina

Reading the Mind of the South

[T]he machine was obviously going
to pieces. . . . The Harrow was not
writing, it was only jabbing, and the
Bed was not turning the body over but
only bringing it up quivering against
the needles.
—Kafka, "In the Penal Colony"

For what is the *Heart*, but a *Spring*;
and the *Nerves*, but so many *Strings*;
and the *Joynts*, but so many *Wheeles*,
giving motion to the whole Body, such
as was intended by the Artificer?
—Thomas Hobbes, *Leviathan*

Recently, meditating about poetry and about issues of personal and cultural history generally and class in the American South particularly, I had an urge to look back at W. J. Cash's classic *The Mind of the South*. But when I went to my bookshelf, I found that the book, like so many others, had unaccountably vanished.

"Oh, no," I thought, "*The Mind of the South* is lost!" Convinced that *The Mind of the South* could be bought cheaply, I went to a large used bookstore and asked for it. "*The Mind of the South*," said the helpful cashier. "Would that be folklore?"

Badoom-boom went the vaudeville drummer who works the comedy club at the back of my medulla oblongata. But in the small city in western Oregon where I was then living, only I heard it. "No," I told the cashier, suddenly caught in my own Spenglerian irony, "*The Mind of the South* is history."

And that is where I found it, on the shelf with Devoto's *Course of Empire*, Tocqueville's *Democracy in America*, and Gary Wills's *Under God: Religion and American Politics*. But yes, I kept thinking, *The Mind of the South* would be folklore: would be, *would* be. Pointless to bring up any of this with the cashier; it takes a connoisseur to blush at classism as subtle as that.

Since I was born and reared in the southeastern region of the United States of North America—and since my people, as they say in those parts, were born and reared there too, and their people before them—I am part of what we talk about when we talk about the mind of the South. My father is a Mississippian; my mother is a Mississippian displaced from Louisiana. My father's family, past and present, is made up of people who are intelligent and not proud of it, inflexible and not worried about it, with minds at once narrow and deep; below-out-of-sight serfs, they immigrated from farms in Bavaria in the late nineteenth century, bought farms cheap in the United States, married farmers, and gave birth to farmers. My mother's people, on the other hand, are bright, mercurial failures; having lived southern for generations out of mind, they possess a history of lost minor wealth, a present of white-collar jobs, a future of inertia, and a keen sense of irony. By the late 1930s, when my parents met, it was clear enough that my father's family had transcended its origin and was rising toward middle class and that my mother's family was in gradual, but considerable, decline. Their marriage inscribed a neat intersection of socioeconomic

graph lines, and at that particular statistical crossroad, I was conceived and birthed.

Histories, bloodlines, appropriations, decline, fall, earth: Any
meditation about poetry and class in the South has to start in such
rhetorical territory. For me, the central question is whether it also
has to end there. Thinking about things southern makes me irri-
table; my eyes narrow, and my skin begins itching. I do not like to
revisit these issues. I do not like to resurrect these conventions. If I
say, like Faulkner's Quentin Compson, that I do not hate the South,
that is supposed to signify its opposite. What, then, if I say of the
South that I do not love it?

And yet, when I meet the automatic assumption—mechanical,
bourgeois, sublime—that the mind of the South can only be folk-
loric, that Br'er Rabbit is the South's best spokescreature, I begin to
itch in other ways. Like anyone, I can pretend to ignore my history
only at my peril; at the same time, I cannot afford to be simple-
minded about it. Particularly among white southerners such as myself, however apostate, southern-think is a powerful mental machinery, a device of meshed metaphors and narrative patterns that one
tends either to accept or to deny entirely because it is so difficult to
dismantle. But I am convinced—to mix a metaphor as precisely as
possible—that only in the innermost workings of that machine can
I find the ghost to which my past requires me to offer up my bowl of
goat's blood.

The summer of 1965, the year I turned fifteen, I spent my time
driving a combine, working my uncle's farm, where many acres had
been devoted to a diabolical crop known as the wild winter pea.

Wild winter peas are mostly useless. The pea itself, about the
same size and hardness as a black BB, is toxic. If cattle eat the pea,
my uncle told me, it makes them sick; if they eat enough of them—
which they will do, given a chance—they die. If birds eat wild winter
peas—and they often do, gathering in great numbers around grain
bins, attracted by the abundant spillage—they become desperately

drunk. This was of great interest to me and to the other farmhands; we would stop by the bins at sunset, on our way home from the fields, and watch droves of blitzed doves stagger foolishly, grounded. They were easy to catch; once you had one in your hands, you could feel how completely it had glutted itself, its gullet stuffed and gravelly like a beanbag. Some of us caught them and let them go; some of us snapped their necks and took home as many as we could catch. Doves, even drunk, make a good meal.

My uncle grew wild winter peas because a government farm subsidy program paid him to grow them. In the winter, the wild winter pea made a decent cover crop and reasonably good cold-weather grazing, green like winter wheat through the dead months. But in the spring it became a dense vine, and by early summer, when the peas themselves appeared, its vegetation covered the earth in an impenetrable waist-high tangle. This was the stuff we were supposed to harvest—in spite of the fact that the pea itself was good for nothing but seed. Farmers were paid by the government to grow a product that was only good to sell to other farmers to produce more of the same product, thus using otherwise fertile land to do essentially nothing. The net result, theoretically, was to reduce the production of genuinely useful crops (cotton, corn, sorghum, and soybeans) and keep prices high. My uncle was granted an acreage allotment on which he could grow "real" crops; the rest of his land was given over to the wild winter pea.

I became a combineer that summer by default. A couple of years before, my older brother and my cousin, both of them mechanically minded people, bought a down-and-out Massey-Harris combine, worked a miracle of repair on its engine and harvesting mechanism, and went into the freelance harvesting business. This enterprise was considered exemplary by my parents, my uncle, and the other farmers in the neighborhood for whom my brother and cousin worked; in fact, the two of them made a local reputation for themselves as agricultural wünderkinder, young Edisons of farm entrepreneurship. Never mind that the Massey-Harris machine was small and outmoded and prone to disastrous breakdown; the fact that they had saved the money to buy it, had done all the repair work, and had put themselves in business made them local celebrities.

In 1963 and 1964, their last two years of high school, they did a flourishing business, working for my uncle and for other farmers not for wages but for a straight share of the crop they harvested. One-tenth of everything they combined was theirs, and they sold their share to brokers just as all the other farmers did. They had become, at a stroke, farmers, businessmen, and technicians. With two of them to drive and service the one machine, they made a fair amount of money—enough to make a hefty contribution toward their educations at the nearby agricultural and engineering university. The business was so lucrative, in fact, that in the summer of 1965, when they both wanted to take summer classes at State, they did not care to do without the money they made from the Massey-Harris; and so, after some negotiation, we agreed that I would take over as driver, with the understanding that we would all share the income equally, each taking a third of a tenth of what the combine harvested.

In spite of the scrupulous equality of the division, I wasn't really a full partner in the business. For one thing, I didn't own a share of the Massey-Harris, and thus I had no responsibility to pay for its upkeep; but because I had no replacement driver, I had to spend more time behind the wheel than either of them ever had, so that made it fair to split the income in straight percentages. Clearly, I was hired help, labor and not management. And nobody thought it should be otherwise, least of all me.

In Kafka's "In the Penal Colony," a character known only as "the condemned man" is executed for an unknown crime. He is written to death on a mechanism known as "the machine," which consists of two parts: the Bed, on which the condemned is restrained, and the Harrow, whose function ought to be self-explanatory. "[T]he Bed vibrated," Kafka tells us, "the needles flickered above the skin, the Harrow rose and fell." Kafka's language is curiously agricultural, "harrow" and "bed" delineating, among other things, images of cultivation: the implement that rips, the earth that receives. Like so many of Kafka's curious existential/allegorical images, this is a multivalent creation—perhaps it is a metaphor for art, but then again, perhaps it more adequately analogizes the action of a society on its members, the character of a culture incised—materially, through language—on the bodies of its citizens.

For certain astrologers, the universe is a vast, etherial clockwork, a machine stamping its influence on souls like a die press on sheet steel. I carry with me the superstition—a materialist or mechanistic version of astrology, perhaps, or a twentieth-century-American misreading of the doctrine of the karmic turbine—that a person is stamped forever by the character of what surrounds him or her at the moment of birth. This passes in me for what writers so often call "a sense of place."

Given its character and mine, Macon, Mississippi, the town where I was born, must have exerted a particularly unfortunate complex of influences. It was, as I remember it from the dawn of my consciousness in the mid-1950s, mean and ugly. Storefronts had lost whatever original character they might have had in the postwar passion for glass and sheet-metal facades. There were hardware stores full of bolts, lead pipe, wrenches, plumbers' aids, and copper wiring; there were two banks containing identical currency and loan applications; there was a store that was known as "The Bookstore," even though it contained no books but traded instead in slick and pulp magazines, stationery, ballpoint pens, and toys; there were two automobile dealerships (Ford and Chevrolet) and several gas stations (Pure Oil, Gulf, Texaco); there was a courthouse, a jail, a health clinic, a tiny desperate library; there was a garment factory, a Double Cola bottling plant, a cotton gin. Even the few finer houses on the north side of town—antebellum reconstructions—only served to intensify the deadness of the rest of it. It was all unremarkable, a twentieth-century cliché.

Providing real proof of its character would require me to make an omniscient catalog of that place, the town and the countryside surrounding it—like Whitman squared and cubed, a treatment of a whole county as complete as James Agee gives the Gudgers' bedroom in *Let Us Now Praise Famous Men*. What a terrible vision that would be, what an enormity of visionary dreariness: a landscape of rust, of semiabandoned storefronts and neglected backstreets, of disemboweled engines, of hayhooks and harrows, dead cattle, sheet-tin galvanized rooftops, pickup trucks and beer cans, silos and hay barns and outhouses, fire ants and cottonmouths, rednecks and tenant farmers and quasi-aristocrats, dogs living and dead, cats wild and tame, and a lot of children wandering through the contours of that countryside wondering, "What the hell is this?"

That vision, however real, is too grim and shapeless to serve any meditation. Imagine instead a gigantic robot tractor moving across a muddy field, its wheels pressing volumes of mud beneath it—pieces of flat-pressed clay, each scrap bearing a fragmentary impression of the machine's treads. Assume that each of those bits of accidentally shaped mud is a consciousness. What will such a consciousness imagine itself to be?

It will notice that it has shape.

It will surmise that the rubble in the midst of which it discovers itself has some meaning.

It will imagine that its shape is a wholeness, or that its shape is the *image* of a wholeness, like the image reflected by a fragment of a mirror, or that its shape is a *particle* of a wholeness, like a jigsaw puzzle piece, and that the other fragments that surround it are the other pieces that, reassembled, would make a complete picture.

It will have no notion whatever of the tractor, which by now will be long beyond the horizon and out of sight.

If it ever begins—looking at its situation in the cold light of day and feeling the beginning of a terrible suspicion—to *imagine* the agency that has given it form, what name would it give its fiction of the tractor?

What difference would it make?

It has been often remarked that the word "verse," which applies at core to a *line* of poetry, comes from the Old English word "fers," which means to plow a furrow and derived from the Latin "versus," which originally means the turning point, when the plowman reaches the end of the row and turns back to begin again. From the *New Shorter OED*: "verse . . . *n.* [OE *fers* corresp. to OFris. *fers*, MLG, OHG (Du., G.), ON *vers*, f. L *versus* turn of the plough, furrow, line, row, line of writing.]"

That I grew up a farmer among farmers is fundamental to my thinking about poetry. They were people who understood plowing. They knew *fers*, then, and they knew *versus*. On the other hand, they didn't know a damn thing about verse, and none of them ever taught me how to plow.

Unlike my brother, I had never shown any aptitude for things mechanical; I was considered, with good reason, a klutz with tools. Our family has a heavy dose of Teutonic genes, and many of my relatives inherited what appears to be an effortless gift at practical engineering. I received none of that instinct, and living among those so endowed, I was a sort of idiot, like a bad dancer in a family of ballerinas—loved and tolerated and worried about. It was the tail end of the great mid-twentieth-century age of engineering, the last gasp of the Sputnik era, and out of it as I was, I was despaired of. I despaired of myself. How could such a person be entrusted with so vitally important a job as plowing?

Clumsily disguised to myself as a white boy, I had suspicion and very little else as my mental equipment. I was born in that small east-central Mississippi town on August 7, 1950, in a hospital that no longer exists as a hospital. It is now an apartment building; the room in which my mother lay unconscious (in the medical manner of the 1950s) during her labor has now become something mundane and utilitarian—a kitchen, a living room, a bathroom. A stove probably memorializes the spot where I first saw light, perhaps a television set, somebody's easy chair, or a toilet.

I know that my mother was unconscious during my birth because she has told me so—with regret, particularly when my now-ex-wife and I were going through Lamaze training for "natural" childbirth. My mother has told me that even after having two children, she was still more or less in the dark about the mechanics of the birthing process, at least in its details; obviously, she remembers nothing of either delivery. She submitted herself, more or less unquestioningly, I think, to the mechanics of birth, about which she knew little, mediated by a set of medical procedures about which she was told next to nothing—a double mystery, twice. She was presented the first time with my brother and the second time with me.

As in most things in the life of my family generally, I was more problematic in my arrival than was my brother, though in this one instance, at least, I can't be blamed. My parents have different blood polarities—my mother's is Rh-negative, my father's Rh-positive. These days that's not much of a problem; there are relatively simple medical remedies. In 1950 that wasn't the case. Then, there would usually be no difficulty in bringing the first child to term, but with subsequent children the risk increased exponentially because of the antibodies the mother had developed during her first pregnancy. A second or later child often did not survive. My birth, I gather from thirdhand reports, was not easy.

I have in my mind an imaginatively constructed image of that delivery room in a fifth-rate hospital in Macon, Mississippi, where my mother lay on a delivery table, with her feet up in the stirrups, unconscious. It was August in Mississippi, ninety-nine degrees, 99 percent humidity, no air conditioning. I imagine sweat beaded on the balding forehead of the doctor, sweat runnelling the faces of the nurses (I see two, one white and one black). The delivery room I create is small and a little shabby, as befits a future bathroom. It was painted medicinal institutional green before the Second World War and is now badly in need of repainting, but why bother if you're the head physician and you *own* the goddamned hospital—if you already have plans to build another, bigger one on the other side of town and turn this place into a toilet? There is stainless steel; there's a scalpel. Episiotomy? Why not? The patient is knocked out anyway—make it easy on the doctor.

And there is my mother, disastrously and angelically unconscious, draped from the waist up, sweating, and streaked with amni-
otic fluid and blood from the waist down. What does she know?
She's twenty-six years old; she never went to college. They gave her a
powerful drug. How can she defend herself? She's not only been
kept ignorant; she's entirely out of it, gone. And yet she's beautiful
there on the table if you know how to see under the sweat and under
the strain that shows even through general anesthetic. And sooner
or later, out of all that stainless steel and gleaming body fluid—it's
astonishing how much liquid comes out of the womb during birth; I
saw it when my daughter was born—I emerge, blue, clashing with
that terrible old traditional green, already loving my mother with the
fierce, selfish, absolutely unconscious and completely intractable
love that is nothing more than the sheer will of the flesh to live and
at all costs to live forever.

The word "prosody" is generally understood as having come from
Greek, *ode* [song] plus *pros* [toward]: a moving toward song. However, I prefer to think of *pros-* also in another way: "against," as to
move toward something until you come right up against it (as in
"prostrate"). I realize that to think of "prosody" as meaning "to come
up against song" is idiosyncratic, but I find that definition useful. So
lovers, for instance, face to face—with each other as with their own
situations and perhaps with their guilt—"come up against song."
No, I'm not against evil, goes the old joke; I wouldn't get that close to
it. This is the root of carpe diem poetry; it is also the root of the blues.

As every songwriter and every poet knows, there's a place where
song and *sense* don't jibe. You have in mind to write a complicated
narrative about your grandmother and her lover and a gasoline
truck and the rain and several dogs, but the music just won't accom-
modate all that and still be music. So, in order to fit it into a twelve-
bar blues form, which is what you feel you have to write because
your cultural posture and circumstances point you that way, you
leave out the grandmother and the rain and just write about the
lover, one of the dogs, and the gasoline truck. You'd rather write

about the lover than the truck, but you want what rhymes with "truck." (Some experts are of the opinion that the etymologically untraceable word "fuck" probably comes from an Old English word meaning "to plow.") So writing the song is a verse-by-verse line of reversals, a compromise between narrative and lyric, between information and harmonious noise. The product is the result of a vector, of the story's having more or less survived a "coming up against song," of the music's having survived the impure roughing-up the facts insist on.

Song, in fact, is the reason I was out on that combine in the summer of 1965. If my take for the season amounted to $350, I could buy a good secondhand electric guitar. All that stood in my way was a thousand acres of wild winter peas.

Machinery, though, was the essential problem: gears, bolts, belts, the complex prosody of the combine. For years, I believed that I was constitutionally incapable of concentrating on details. This, I told myself, was the root of my lack of mechanical skill. I could not really focus on a wrench, much less any job a wrench might have to do. My mind wandered, I became clumsy, and then those gracefully intuitive engineers in my family would groan with impatience and snatch the thing out of my hands. To get even, I tried to turn myself into a musician. I did not understand until years later that music was a means of revenge. Sentimentally, I thought it was my destiny. I was not designed to be a mechanic; I was, instead, an artist—thus ipso facto above all that. Just where I came by such a breached vision I cannot say; music would eventually teach me not only how wrong I was about the difference between the class of the artist and the class of the worker, but also how stupid I could be about the power of patience with detail. A guitar, after all, is a kind of glorified wrench; if you don't know how to hold it, you never get anywhere. And the wrench that is language is a mighty lever, a potent loosener and tightener.

Real proof of contentions about landscapes, regions, places, small-town America, anybody's sacred home ground, always requires a powerful rhetoric of detail—unless the contentions are sentimental ones, which by definition require no proof at all. By the time I was fifteen years old, I had collected plenty of sentimental contentions about the place in which I was growing up. That summer, driving my brother's combine, I began to subject myself to the discipline of proof, the rhetoric of detail.

Operating a large and serious machine requires attention to detail. A machine, in fact, is nothing but a collection of details, minutiae meshed together. This is especially true of combines, which are not sleek and sophisticated creations. A combine is an absurd Rube Goldberg gadget, a great rumbling shambling example of the sheer power of the counterintuitive. Nothing about the construction of a combine is what a sane human being would expect. A combine is not mysteriously complex, like the cosmos of the old astrologers; a combine is inelegantly complicated. A combine spits in the eye of physicists, who are in love with law, beauty, and charm. A combine rattles and roars; a combine vibrates and stumbles as it goes; a combine devours and farts; a combine, inevitably, breaks down.

To learn my stuff as a combineer, I had warmed up on wheat. Wheat is an easy crop to combine; all you really have to harvest are the heads, and those are high off the ground. The driver raises and lowers a combine's header—the front end, where the business of cutting goes on—by means of a complex hydraulic system controlled by levers. With wheat, keeping the header at the right height is simple. Also, wheat stalks are quite easy for a combine's cutter bar—the leading edge of the machine, a double row of triangular steel blades that clip like monstrous pinking shears—to deal with. The wheat is dry when you harvest it; the stalks are brittle, and the wheat stalk is structurally uncomplicated. Because it was still late May when the wheat harvest started, my brother was there to walk me through it. It was easy. I logged enough hours to earn the removal of my combineer's training wheels, and we were in business.

Wheat fields are legendary, mythic: amber waves and all the conceptual baggage thereof. Wild winter peas have, as far as I know, no connotations, and certainly, when they are ready for harvest, no aesthetic appeal. In winter, they *are* green like wheat, pretty against the dead landscape; in the spring, when the vines are dilating, they produce a small and not unpretty violet flower. By June they've gone to seed and the vines are dead. A wild winter pea field ready for combining is a waist-deep chaos of organic cable. Even dried, the vines are pithy and tough; they are also prodigiously voluminous. And the pea pods—full of those poisonous BBs that would yield up my precious third of a tenth—are not handily located at the top. There *is* no top. The pods grow along the length of the vine; the vine winds and curls back on itself, weaves in and out of its own mass. The vines may lift their pods two feet off the ground or lay them *on* the ground. The upshot is that the vine in its labyrinthine entirety has to go through the combine; anything the combine misses is waste.

Imagine trying to cram a thousand acres of baling wire down your throat.

"With peas," my brother had advised me, "you want to keep the header very low, no more than an inch off the ground." The hours I logged harvesting wheat had not prepared me for the demands of this requirement. The difficulty—as I learned instantly when I actually began combining peas—is that the earth is not flat. A combine will quickly teach you that the earth is a chaotic complex of geometries, disturbed not only by its own vague chthonic inclinations but also by the aggregated industries of crawfish, fire ants, and human beings. A crawfish chimney can jam a cutter bar; a fire ant mound three feet high, hidden like a Mayan ruin in the jungle of pea vines, can stall a whole combine—and then, if you're the driver, you have to clear away the mess, remembering that enough fire ant bites can kill a child or a calf.

But the most dangerous obstacle of all, the most insidious and profound, is the abandoned turn row. Plowing a field moves soil, and where the plow turns—the enjambment, the "versus" of the "fers"—it collects like sediment at the mouth of a river. Years of plowing a piece of land establishes distinct ridges along these lines of demarcation: turn rows.

Archaeologists say that the most permanent way to mark the earth is to dig a hole; its traces remain forever. I would argue that the second most permanent mark you can make is to raise a turn row. The land I was harvesting had been tilled for generations, but recently the fields had changed their boundaries; as the economy moved farming from family subsistence to agribusiness, from labor intensive to machine dominated, fields had grown larger. The turn rows, however, remained permanent; agriculture's speed bumps, they were permanent testimony of the labor of farmhands long dead, of vanished families, of quaint old John Deeres long gone to the rust heap, of mules rendered into glue generations ago. Invisible underneath acres of pea-tangle, the old turn rows waited to warp my header, to stall my machine, to bend me, to break me, to tip me over. After a while, lousy mechanic but budding prosodist, I began to memorize those abandoned line breaks and to intuit their presence even though I could not see them. Arbitrary and ineradicable as blank verse, they made themselves felt.

The poem, insists William Carlos Williams, meaning something else entirely, is a field. Yes: and *no ideas but in things.*

W. J. Cash's *Mind of the South* appeared in 1941, the same year as F. O. Matthiessen's *American Renaissance*, and it is to southern cultural history what Matthiessen's book is to the study of American literature. Brilliant, passionate, monumental—and, like many monuments, outdated and vaguely embarrassing—each book is a testament to a love affair with history so intense that on some level it is illicit. Cash is the South's answer to Matthiessen right down to the fact of his suicide; in an odd way he is also the South's answer to Hart Crane, insofar as his death, like Crane's, involved a Guggenheim Fellowship, a journey to Mexico City, a superintense fascina-

tion with America, alcohol, and, paradoxically, the hope of a significant new relationship. Cash, Matthiessen, and Crane are similar in
their obsessions, three wild winter peas rattling in the brittle pod of
American Romanticism. Bertram Wyatt-Brown, who wrote the introduction ("The Mind of W. J. Cash") to Vintage's 1991 reissue of
The Mind of the South, informs us that

> In *Southern Politics in State and Nation* (1949), V. O. Key, Jr., observed
> that "a depressingly high rate of self-destruction prevails among
> those who ponder about the South and put down their reflections in
> books. A fatal frustration seems to come from the struggle to find a
> way through the unfathomable maze formed by tradition, caste,
> race, poverty." Key probably had in mind Jack Cash. (xxxiii)

Manic-depressive, ingenious, driven, Cash imprints the floor plan
of his version of that maze on everyone who comes to ponder the
myth of the South seriously.

Cash asserts, "[T]he Old South may be said, in truth, to have been
nearly innocent of the notion of class in any rigid and complete
sense," but at the same time he claims that "nowhere else in
America, indeed, not forgetting even Boston, would class awareness
in a certain very narrow sense figure so largely in the private thinking of the master group" (34). The thread that leads to the Minotaur
in the maze is an understanding of the South's uncanny ability to
blur the distinctions between "caste" and race while remaining
largely unaware of the mental machinations necessary to carry out
such an operation:

> If the plantation had introduced distinctions of wealth and rank
> among the [white] men of the old backcountry, and, in doing so, had
> perhaps offended against the ego of the common white, it had also,
> you will remember, introduced that other vastly ego-warming and
> ego-expanding distinction between the white man and the black.
> Robbing him and degrading him in so many ways, it yet, by singu-
> lar irony, had simultaneously elevated this common white to a posi-

tion comparable to that of, say, the Doric knight of ancient Sparta. Not only was he not exploited directly, he was himself made by extension a member of the dominant class—was lodged solidly on a tremendous superiority, which, however much the blacks in the "big house" might sneer at him, and however much their masters might privately agree with them, he could never publicly lose. Come what might, he would always be a white man. And before that vast and capacious distinction, all others were foreshortened, dwarfed, and all but obliterated.

The grand outcome was the almost complete disappearance of economic and social focus on the part of the [white] masses. (38–39)

A Marxist might have rendered this more plainly but not more tragically: false consciousness, the natural affinity of laborers in similar circumstances obliterated, *awareness* of class warped in the service of maintaining class tyranny. In the end, for better or worse, Cash speaks as a white man who has lived the southern experience and is in love with it no matter how its deceits and enormities torture him. "Was there ever another instance of a country," Cash asks in bewildered admiration,

in which the relation of master and man arose, negligible exceptions aside, only with reference to a special alien group—in which virtually the whole body of the [white] natives who had failed economically got off fully from the servitude that, in one form or another, has almost universally been the penalty of such failure—in which they were *parked*, as it were, and left to go to the devil in the absolute enjoyment of their liberty?

Answering his own question in advance, Cash begins this paragraph by declaring, "In this regard, it seems to me, the Old South was one of the most remarkable societies which ever existed in the world" (37).

The combine was a patchwork leviathan. It rumbled and smoked and fell apart, and yet it took out an eight-foot swath of field with every pass. It harvested. I sat on the platform ten feet off the ground, breathing an acre of dust a day—this was before cabs and air conditioning—moving the header up and down by hydraulic increments, watching as best I could for all the devils of the field that wanted to bring me down. Driving a combine was a practical course in paying attention. When the cylinder choked on pea vines, as it did every half hour or so, I stopped, shut the engine down, and forced the clog through, levering the mechanism with a four-foot iron pipe. When something broke, I fixed it as best I could. The alternative was to quit work and lose an hour or a day of combining time. And every wild winter pea that landed in the hopper was a molecule of a solid-body electric rhythm and blues guitar.

The truth is that no matter how hard I worked that summer— and I worked my tail off—it was all a kind of luxury. Every penny I made, I could spend however I wanted, and when the harvest was done and September came around, I was through. No matter that W. J. Cash's Old South was (exactly) a century dead and gone; no matter that Reconstruction was over and the Bulldozer Era was enlarging pea fields and opening the embryonic Sunbelt's parking lots: Come what might, in the mind of the South I would always be a white man. And in Noxubee County, Mississippi, in 1965, that meant about the same thing it had meant in Cash's prelapsarian Virginia. All the clichés of southern apartheid still held, the psychic turn rows of a vanishing subculture. Jim Crow sat in the courthouse; public drinking fountains were still labeled "white" and "colored," in defiance of federal court orders (and yes, just like the books say, when I was three years old, I expected rainbow water to come out of the obvious spigot); and my high school was resolutely and absolutely segregated the entire time I attended, in spite of the fact that the population of the county was something like 70 percent black.

If there was a fundamental difference between my South and the one Cash describes in *The Mind of the South*, it was a pervading certainty of belatedness. In 1965 things were more or less pragmatically as they had been in terms of race and class; yet the handwriting was on the wall, and everybody knew it, no matter what we might have said to each other while we watched the civil rights movement on the evening news. One immediate consequence of this blessed fatalism was that at least for a time, the color line grew more intense and serious, more absolute, more uncrossable. The mask had begun to slip; as actual enforcement of federal court rulings penetrated deeper and deeper into the heartland (we were among the deepest), folks drew back and waited.

From the platform of the combine where I sweated and swore, it was four hundred miles to Dallas, Texas, and the grassy knoll, and only forty miles to Philadelphia, Mississippi, where three civil rights workers had been murdered not long before. It could have happened anywhere, you might say, but what I knew at the time was that it had happened in my own backyard. Little Rock, Atlanta, Jackson State, Selma: The movement lit up names all around us, and if for the moment the latest model of W. J. Cash's Old South Machine was still hitting on all cylinders, there could be no doubt that the engine was about to blow.

So if on a summer evening I took my alto saxophone—the first instrument I had learned to love—out on the back porch to practice my lame instrumental imitations of "Louie, Louie" and "Be Bop a Lula" or (much better) the horn licks from "Midnight Hour" and "Knock on Wood," and if I should hear, as I sometimes did, an answering electric guitar riff from a tenant farmer's house on the next farm, I was forbidden to cross that mile of empty field, sit down on the porch, and say, "Hey, man, show me how you did that." My people, steamrollered by the leviathan of the Old South and the New, were racists; they raised me a racist. They forbade me; I forbade myself.

The mind of the South is history.

What was class in rural Mississippi in the 1950s and early '60s when I was a boy? It was land; it was time; it was money to some degree; above all, it was race.

Class one, the aristocrats, were those who lived on land they owned and that had been owned by their families for generations, yea even back to the Old South. They might have money or they might not, but if they were white, owned land, and could trace their ancestry back far enough, they were royalty.

Take away the history and you have class two: people who were white and owned land. This is where my family fell—German immigrants on my father's side, down-and-out Louisiana bourgeois on my mother's, we owned a modest farm. My earliest experiences are those of an archetypal farm boy: dairy, barnyard, and garden were my regions, the usual chores my duty. Though we never moved off the farm, by the late 1950s my father was no longer a farmer; he had become a civil servant working for the Postal Service. But that signified nothing. We lived on land we owned, and we were white. If we had lived in a northern city on the same income and with the same professional status, we would have been lower middle class, one degree (recently removed) above working class. In rural Mississippi we occupied a sort of pale nouveau lower lordship—if not quite "elevated . . . to a position comparable to that of, say, the Doric knight of ancient Sparta," as Cash puts it, certainly given more than our earned due.

Take away the land and you have class three.

Take away whiteness and you have the rest.

W. J. Cash, in the passage cited above, laid bare the meaning of the mechanism whereby class and race—in the Old South, and still in the South of the mid-1950s—were blurred so precisely. For him, this mechanism was an occasion for a kind of horrified wonder; for others of us, it was more bleak and brutal than that.

A memory: It's a fall day, 1955 or so, probably a Saturday afternoon, and my father has taken me out on the farm to watch him hunt rabbits.

I wonder, now, why my father did this. He was never much of a rabbit hunter; his real love along these lines was quail hunting. But he seemed to feel the need, now and again, to instruct me in such things. And maybe on this particular day he felt some particular restlessness, some need to get out of the house—who knows?

I am about five years old, making my father thirty-three—twenty years younger than I am as I write this. We have been walking over fields a mile or so behind the house, flushing rabbits out of frost-killed grass. My father has his .22 automatic rifle. Too young to shoot, I am present as a spectator only.

I suppose there was some pedagogical purpose. Maybe I was supposed to learn something about the way rabbits behave, which in fact I did learn. Maybe the point was simply to make me accustomed to the concrete fact of killing animals, which I never quite got—partly because of my parents' own ambivalence about having me learn it. But that's another story.

At some point, my father kills a couple of rabbits. When he has done this, he is through, and we head home. Now the truth of the matter is, my father doesn't *want* the rabbits. He doesn't want to clean them, and he doesn't want to eat them. On the whole, my father is not a man who hunts *just* to kill—he's not a sportsman but a practical hunter, he tells himself, who eats what he kills. (He comes out of a tradition of people who hunt for meat of necessity, but he has ceased to be such a person.) So now he has a dilemma— what to do with these rabbits. He doesn't want to throw them away; that would offend his sense of propriety. He doesn't want to feed them to his dogs; trained bird dogs, they shouldn't get the taste for "varmint," which would distract them from the scent of birds.

About that time we're passing close by a tenant farmer's house— a two-room unpainted tin-roofed shack, in 1955 almost certainly without electricity—where a farmhand named Jim lives with his considerable family. As we pass, we meet a child about my age, one of Jim's children, who is outside playing. My father sees his opportunity and says to the child, "Here, boy, you want these rabbits?"— holding them up.

Already I'm a little startled by what's going on. In the first place, at age five, I've rarely been in the proximity of black children—I've seen them from a distance but never been allowed to approach them. But even more startling, at the moment, is my father's voice. He is speaking in a way I've never heard him speak: he is speaking pure Black English, which he learned as a boy when, unlike me, he grew up associating fairly freely and intimately with black children his own age. What made the difference, from his boyhood to mine, was the certain knowledge that the blurred boundaries of southern class and race relations were in the process of being dazzlingly clarified.

The child, seeing the rabbits, is delighted. "Yay," he says.

This, I come quickly to understand, is not shorthand for *hooray*. It's simply Black English for "yes." I figure that one out because instantly my father becomes furious. He raises his hand—the one with the rifle in it, since the other one is full of dead dangled rabbits—and says (again in the purest Mississippi black dialect, which I can't even begin to render with phonetic accuracy here): "Don't you *never* say 'yay' to me, boy. You don't say 'yay' to a white man. You say 'yas*suh*.' You hear me?" Then he drops the rabbits on the ground and we pass on.

But I am deeply shocked by what I have just witnessed. In the first place, I've never seen my father exhibit such anger; he is generally a mild and unemotional man. And he has unleashed this anger on a child of about my own age and size. Furthermore, he has spoken in a voice I've never heard, in a language I've never heard him use. Buttons have been pushed, levers moved; wheels are turning. It's as if there's another—and *dangerous*—presence living inside my father, which I've never known about. An automaton has risen up inside the flesh-and-blood man I no longer know in the way I thought I had. Quite possibly, it seems to me at this moment, if I do or say the wrong thing, that presence may manifest itself against *me*. And for the first time in my life, I am afraid of my father.

W. J. Cash writes of "the influence of the Southern physical world— itself a sort of conspiracy against reality in favor of romance." He has in mind a certain vegetable lushness, or the gloamy haziness of the Smoky Mountains. But the South has many bodies, many material realities. To what extent one gives in to this "conspiracy" depends entirely on one's angle of vision.

My father's exaggerated anger was no doubt in part an improvised pedagogical act, which must have seemed to him completely natural, designed to teach children—the black child and his own son—something about the boundary between black and white languages, black and white people. And it was a reality-obscuring veil: I was made to feel the "romance" of the otherness of this child—but was also made to feel that he and I, as children, were similarly powerless to do anything in the face of the anger of a white adult, and at the same time powerless to do anything about the distance between us. This was all embedded in language, of course—but also in more than language. There was a whole register of symbols, the words, the tone of voice, the shift in tone, the obvious anger, the raised hand with rifle, the rabbits thrown on the ground—even the assumption that black people would welcome the rabbits, food that white people of a certain class would consider marginal.

The black child must learn to fear the white man outside himself; the white child must learn to fear (read "respect") the white man within.

Class, race, subservience, and mastery—or "tradition, caste, race, poverty," as V. O. Keys makes it—were cogs in the wheel that drove the social machine in which I was fostered. My own position in that schematic was prepared for me. However much I dismantle it, however desperately I repudiate it, it is my inheritance. Like Faulkner's Ike McCaslin (*Go Down, Moses*), for years I have worked to disinherit myself. Still, I am at least in part defined by the energy I have expended in the effort.

"Because it was working so silently," Kafka says, "the machine simply escaped one's attention."

The story could—and in fact, in a certain way, does—end there. But in a universe as insistently impure as ours, there is never only one machine at work. Sweating on my brother's combine, I was caught on a turning belt that had an infinitely regressive Möbius twist; harvesting a crop that had no purpose beyond raising another identical crop, I was playing out the drama of my own class destiny. As it turned out, there were other realities: other machines, other fields to sweat in.

Sometime in the early 1980s, I went to a bluegrass festival with a couple of musician friends—bluegrass lovers all of us, but after three days of hearing "Rocky Top" and "Foggy Mountain Breakdown" played by amateurs in every campground at the site, we were hungry for something rawer. "What would happen," one of us said, "if every bluegrass guitar picker in the world played a G chord at the same time?" Not much, we decided. All it would take would be one Muddy Waters playing a Stratocaster through a Fender Twin Reverb amp to blow the whole lot of 'em to kingdom come. That's the kind of apocalypse machine the electric guitar can be.

Though I couldn't have expressed it so at the time, that's what I was working for in the summer of 1965.

It has become a truism of histories of rock 'n' roll music that all through the 1950s and early 1960s, young white musicians took transistor radios to bed with them and, hiding under the sheets, tuned in certain radio stations: WLS in Chicago, WWL in New Orleans, Nashville's WLAC. You had to listen late at night, after hours, when the FCC let these stations turn up to their full cosmos-shaking fifty thousand watts. Then it didn't matter where you were: Toronto, Seattle, Omaha—every part of the continent has produced its artists who tell the same story.

And what were they listening to? You know already, because it has become a part of American folklore. They were tuning in the blues and R&B, everything that used to be subsumed under the heading "race music": Muddy Waters, Big Mama Thornton, Clarence "Frogman" Henry, Wynonie Harris, B. B. King. They listened; it made a difference. And not only to whatever we mean when we say rock 'n' roll.

It came out of machines—out through Lucille, B. B. King's elec-
trified Gibson guitar, through Elmore James's cranked-up amp,
through the vast transmitters of WLS, to a miraculous little
cigarette-sized box you could plug right in your ear so that nobody
could hear it except you—but it was rocking the firmament. You had
to listen late at night because that's when it was on, but it also felt
right to listen then. It was part of the machinery of the night, and
especially for many young white listeners, it was illicit. This was not
music your parents listened to or wanted you to hear. Some of it
(Wynonie Harris's "I Love My Baby's Puddin'") was what we used to
call suggestive; some of it (The Coasters' "Riot in Cell Block #9")
was radical. This music was transgressive and everybody knew it. It
worked like an abrasive wheel on rusty metal. It scoured. It burned.

The blues is an antidote to anything in the mind of the South that
conspires against reality.

Just to provide one prominent example from a distant remove,
Robbie Robertson of The Band—the author of perhaps the most
moving musical tribute to, and exposé of, Cash's Old South, "The
Night They Drove Old Dixie Down"—was listening from a bedroom
in his hometown, Toronto. In an interview for *Across the Great
Divide: The Band and America*, Robertson told Barney Hoskyns that
when he first heard southern music, "I found it so heavy in my heart
that I couldn't get around it, you know." He heard what he has called

the rawest sound, just dirty and up to no good. Dirty to me . . .
meant Bo Diddly and Hubert Sumlin, Howlin' Wolf's guitarist.
They put me over the top. I had no choice but to play guitar. I
wanted to be part of that *sound*. (13–14)

I understand that desire. I shared it in the 1960s, and I share it
still. It's a kind of materialist mysticism, America's favorite kind: to
go out "over the top" through the machinery of rhythm and blues—
Humbucking guitar pickups, Fender amps, and that godlike radio
transmitter—to travel through the atmosphere (exactly like Walt
Whitman in "The Sleepers") and enter all those bedrooms through

transistorized portals. Give me an amplifier big enough, the impulse says, and I'll play a G chord that will blow out the sun. Give me a radio small enough, and I'll become the most intimate whisper you ever heard. Either way, both ways at once, I'll tell you what you most want to hear another human being say. Either way, both ways at once, I'll tell you the true story of humankind. I'll tell you your own name.

This is a lyric impulse. Here we enter the true domain of prosody, if we define prosody as "moving toward song"—or as "the condition of being up against song."

The combine earned me my guitar. I learned to play it, some. In turn, it took me places. It taught me secrets.

What was on the mind of the South in 1965? To know that, you have to tune in to a lot of channels: Fannie Lou Hamer and Aaron Henry, yes, but also Lester Maddox and Ross Barnett—like it or not, it's all part of a whole. The best way to plug in is through the music of the South, which is the most potent artistic force ever unleashed on the world from below the Mason-Dixon line—Mr. Faulkner, with all due respect, be damned.

Greil Marcus, whose *Mystery Train: Images of America in Rock 'n' Roll Music* ought to take its place alongside *The American Renaissance, The Mind of the South,* and *The Bridge* as a work of peculiarly American genius, has splendidly summarized the power of southern music. Describing the part of north Mississippi that produced Elvis Presley—Tupelo, ninety miles north of where I drove my combine—Marcus says,

> It was, as Southern chambers of commerce have never tired of saying, a Land of Contrasts. The fundamental contrast, of course, could not have been more obvious: black and white. Always at the root of Southern fantasy, Southern music, and Southern politics, the black man was poised in the early fifties for an overdue invasion of American life, in fantasy, music, and politics. As the North scurried to deal

with him, the South would be pushed farther and farther into the weirdness and madness its best artists had been trying to exorcise from the time of Poe on down. Its politics would dissolve into night-riding and hysteria; its fantasies would be dull for all their gaudy paranoia. Only the music got away clean. (*Mystery Train* 148)

White musicians owned up to the power of the blues long ago; the other artists of my generation, especially the southern ones, ought to follow suit. The power came in through the radio where I listened after hours; it came in through the air, across our field, from that guitar in the tenant house on the next farm, over the hill. It came in, weakly and clumsily, through my own hands when I tried to learn how B. B. King made *that sound*. It taught me lessons in pain and dignity. It taught me something about a form of expression so far down that it was beyond the thought of money, and at the same time beyond any posturing anticommercial purism. Through the blues, I began to learn that genius is no more mystical than all ordinary life; it is something you sweat for.

Driving my combine, negotiating the prosodic enjambments of my grandfather's turn rows, earning my guitar, I was moving toward song. I was up against song. I was looking for the other side of whatever in my world conspired against reality (which was almost everything). I was after a means to burn that all away. And in the air over that field, it was coming together in ways neither I nor anyone else could hear completely: radio waves, cosmic white noise, the stuttering utterance of black holes, the sound of all the machinery of the universe, including my combine and the guitar on the next farm, where somebody knew how to play Elmore James (a mystery I would never, as a musician, fathom).

"A lyric," according to Daniel Albright,

> is a poem in which one notices a certain shiftiness or instability, a certain slipping and sliding of things, a certain tendency to equate a thing with its antiself, a certain evasiveness of being. In other words, a lyric is magical, and the proper history of the lyric is the history of incantation. (*Lyricality in English Literature* viii)

That was what I heard in, say, Howlin' Wolf (*Smokestack lightnin' / Shining like gold / Don't you hear me calling?*) before I heard the same mysterious resonance in Yeats, Bishop, Brooks, whose voices would reach me by mechanisms at least as covert as transistor radio. I was beginning to learn, that summer, how to listen to the impure, incantatory voices that spoke in the height above our (and every) field, the *versus* above the *fers*. That was the sound I craved, and still crave. If I couldn't get it in one kind of song, I would get it in another.

In the late 1980s, when I was living in England for a year, I heard the Mississippi blues harmonica player Cary Bell—if not exactly a blues great, at least a blues very goddamned good—in a dismal little art bar at the Devon Arts Centre in Exeter. Invited by one of my students, who was a musician in the backup band, to join Bell for a drink between sets, I discovered that he comes from the same place I do, that he grew up in Macon, where I was born, and went to school there. We laughed about it, joking that we had to come to England to get to know each other. We both knew exactly what that meant. And though we made a joke of it, sincerely enough, it broke my heart, and still does, that I never knew Cary Bell when we were both growing up, that I never knew he was in the neighborhood, that I never played the blues with him.

What prevented our meeting then was the machinery of illusion. In the Mississippi of my childhood, the blurred mechanism of race and class conspired to hide what was real from all of us—most particularly to hide the truth about who and what we were. The self-image I was given from birth—incised on the Bed and Harrow of the South—was a lie. Art, then, was a lyric force in Albright's sense: an indeterminate power that sought truth in the form of an antiself.

I find that force, as Albright does, in Auden and Dickinson and Yeats; I also find it, powerfully, in the songs of the great southern musicians—Hank Williams and Jimmie Rodgers, yes, but especially in the practitioners of the blues. They are in the air of American poetry still, as surely as Whitman. We want to be part of that *sound*—raw and impure as a locomotive whistle, descriptive of nightmare and redemption, hopelessness and transcendence.

Robbie Robertson has said that when he first came to the Mississippi Delta from Canada, he realized that this place "was the middle of the wagon of rock 'n' roll. . . . Everything was more musically oriented, and I didn't know if it was coming from the people or just from the air." His colleague from Arkansas, drummer/vocalist Levon Helm, quotes Robertson in *This Wheel's on Fire* as saying that in Arkansas, "people walked in rhythm and talked this singsong talk. . . . When I'd go down by the river in Helena, the *river* seemed to be in rhythm, and I thought, *No wonder this music comes from here: the rhythm is already there.*" The idea that music comes out of air or water—or out of earth, over fields, as it sometimes seemed to me—is mythic, certainly, but like many strong myths it contains its element of truth. Southern music is in fact a sort of antimythology, subversive of the chimera-legends of racism: a counterforce like the psychological warnings that so often come from dreams.

If the music I heard rising across our field evening after evening when I was in my teens was mythic, it was a concrete mythology; it had a local habitation and a name. The man who played on his front porch a mile from my house was Walter Outlaw, who worked days as a sewing machine mechanic in the local garment factory and nights as a sideman in a sixteen-piece band that would play a party for twenty-five dollars. He played a solid Elmore James–flavored blues, using a flat pick and one finger pick, and one night between sets in a rural night club where I was not "supposed" to be, he taught me the rudiments of a tune called "Love in Vain." I bought him a beer and never saw him again.

When the train left the station, it had two lights on behind.
When the train left the station, it had two lights on behind.
The blue light was my blues, the red light was my mind.
All my love's in vain.

This, of course, is the unkillable Robert Johnson, the Keats of the Delta blues, who here embodies Albright's thesis so perfectly that it hardly needs glossing—except to point out that where the incantation of the lyric, for Albright, is the evocation of a magical power that dissolves universes, Robert Johnson's song is about powerlessness. The singer has taken the love of his life to the train station—even carrying her bags for her—so that she can leave him forever. Nothing can erase that loss. And just as he feels the distance opening out—as the mechanical leviathan of the locomotive takes her irrevocably away—one of the most mysterious utterances in human history finds its voice.

In 1976, at the age of twenty-six, I left the South and did not return for exactly twenty years except to visit. I rode that train. I got away, but I did not, like southern music, get away clean. No matter how much we may long to be, people are not pure music, any more than they are pure poetry. I could not get away clean; nobody could.

Considerable periods of time go by when the South, as the South, never enters my consciousness. But insofar as I am a poet, I still depend on two things—possibly complementary, possibly contradictory—that I learned trying to read the mind of the South, one about the labor that is poetry, the other about its heart.

(1) *A poem is a field of action*—W. C. Williams's words, changed by the material reality of my own experience—wherein one labors for all one loves, for the self and the antiself, using all the machinery there is, the combine and the locomotive equally, the upright church piano and the blues guitar. But/and: Insofar as the selfhood I was given as a boy in Mississippi—a child in America—was a deliberate, calculated falsehood, (2) *All my love's in vain.*

Between these poles, everything happens.

The South, old and new, is justly famous for the power of its narratives. The lyric impulse is also an impulse to power: the power to dissolve realities, to void boundaries, to break through human limits. Defined in Albright's terms, racism itself is lyric, insofar as it is a kind of bewitchment that resides, at least in part, in language. The narrative/lyric amalgam of the Old South was an incantation of the rawest power-usurpation, working, as Cash says of the southern landscape, against reality in favor of a romance of mist and violence. That amalgam survived, mutated, into my childhood, and it survives still as one very characteristic chapter of the unfolding memoir of this nation. To this day it echoes in the mind of the South and in the mind of every southerner, black or white, and in the mind of every American.

Misused, lyricism is sheer mystification.

The blues, on the other hand, is a counterspell, a powerful lyric about powerlessness, wedded to a narrative strain that is instinctively occluded because its substance has to be subterranean. *Versus* to the *fers* incised by the Harrow of the white South, the blues is transgressive to the bone. It is a clogging inertia thrown into the augers of force—listen carefully to B. B. King's "Why I Sing the Blues" while imagining cramming a thousand acres of baling wire down your throat—and at the same time a liberating energy. It is exactly what Daniel Albright means when he describes the lyric as

> a swerving aside, a lifting at right angles from the usual axis of narrative or logical discourse. . . . Whenever we read a text and say to ourselves *Something is missing*, whether that something is a recognizably human author, or a customary world representation, or simply sense, we are in the domain of the lyric.

"The blue light was my blues, the red light was my mind": The first time I heard those words, I entered the domain of poetry and never returned.

How far do you have to travel to bridge the distance this phrase describes, its horrendous and surgically precise division? To the other side of the field? To Oregon? To England? To the moon? Who has the power to stop locomotives—or lovers, when they choose to ride them, or young men and women, disaffected, estranged from themselves, needing expatriation? What is the blues if, even though it's "my" blues, it is clearly separate from "my mind"?

Would that be the mind of the South?

Would that be folklore?

Revenge of the American Leviathan

Our high-tech weapons worked, and . . .
[have] changed the face of modern war.
—Lt. Gen. Thomas Kelly, U.S. Army,
Pentagon briefing, February 28, 1991

It walks, it talks, it crawls on its belly
like a reptile.
—Carnival barker's spiel

The bite of conscience . . . is obscene.
—Nietzsche, *On the Genealogy of Morals*

During the night of January 1, 1991, I had a dream, which
I recorded the following morning:

I am in a house that I know to be surrounded by soldiers who are
very dangerous. I have no idea what they are up to, but have no
doubt they will kill me if they find me. There is nowhere to hide. I
am lying facedown on a sofa in a small room, trying to be incon-
spicuous. Suddenly one of the soldiers appears at the door. I have an

impression of him, though from where I am it must be impossible for me actually to see him: a man in special services uniform (camouflage gear, a beret, bandoliers, hand grenades on his belt, an automatic weapon at the ready). I am defenseless; I try to pretend I am dead, but he knows I am not. He shoots me through the back of the head. There is terror but no pain. Am I dead? I can't tell. Somehow I am still conscious, but I am shot through the brain. I must surely either be dead or dying. It seems as if I lie there for a very long time in a strange state of numb and confused detachment while armed men ransack the house and shoot any "enemies" they can find, but I also seem to wake up immediately, in a panic.

Though after-the-fact impressions of dreams are always suspect, what I retained on waking was the chilling memory of how *inevitable* it all seemed, how helpless I was, both before and after being shot, and the "numb and confused detachment" under the spell of which I lay facedown on the sofa, perfectly aware all the while of everything that was going on in the house.

I was to reexperience the same emotions soon. I don't believe that dreams are prophetic—at least not mine—but I am convinced of the sensitivity of the unconscious mind to every nuance of its environment, and on January 1 I was all too consciously aware of what was in the air. Just over two weeks later, on January 16, 1991, at 8:10 p.m., I tore myself away from my television long enough to find a legal pad so that I could write the following:

At 6:58 [EST] this evening—exactly at the end of the *MacNeil-Lehrer NewsHour*—it was announced that war with Iraq had begun. For the past hour, then, with feelings of overwhelming horror and outrage, I've been watching the (not in a good sense) incredible news coverage of the bombing of Iraq.

So far, there have been no reports from Kuwait. So far there are no reports of counterattacks by the Iraqis. So far, Israel is not in the war.

Wave after wave—it's reported—of aircraft are attacking Baghdad. Somehow the reports from the CNN reporters—in a hotel at the city center—continue. It would be impossible to orchestrate a better media event.

"Clearly I've never been there," one reporter says, "but this feels like being at the center of hell."

There is a complete breakdown of conscience.

I stopped writing, feeling the falseness of every word I penned (however "true," in some sense, the facts I was recording may or may not have been). It was as if I were gesticulating in front of a mirror to reassure myself that I had the capacity to feel a certain way, when in fact what I felt was something quite different. I seemed to be lying again on that sofa in my dream, facedown, numb, confused, and detached: not yet understanding that what I was feeling was the beginning, the instinctive denial phase, of a terrible guilty grief.

But the grief I was then beginning to feel—which I also feel as I write now—was of a peculiar kind. Unlike more immediate and personal varieties of grief that most often follow loss, it was first and foremost intellectual. Hence the unconvincingness (even to me, even at the time I wrote it) of the passage above: I knew that I *ought* to be feeling horror and outrage, when what I felt was numbness and confused detachment. I was struggling, unsuccessfully, to find a context for my emotions. Like my dream self, shot in the back of the head and facedown on the sofa, I was experiencing something unprecedented.

Because I am a writer, my first impulse, in the face of a situation that seemed completely wrongheaded, ugly, and dangerous, was to write. That is why, at 8:10 on January 16, I picked up a pen and a legal pad: almost through force of habit. If at 8:20 or so I chose to put the pen and pad away again, it was because the gesture I was making as a writer was a false one. I did not know enough—I did not yet feel clearly enough—to make an effective instrument of writing.

Looking back on that situation, I wonder again what a writer is for. Most of the time, I can delude myself into believing that I know the answer: "A writer is for writing," I might tell myself when I'm feeling tautological; or, when more ethically inclined, "A writer's purpose is the same as the purpose of other human beings—to resist one's own worst impulses, to live a constructive life, and to try whenever possible to help, or persuade, others to do the same." Sometimes, though, other answers seem more likely. At my most despairing—and the war in Iraq and its aftermath have sorely tempted this side of me—I tend to believe that a writer as an artist is nothing more, or less, than a person who has chosen to play a game that is less harmful, less potentially destructive, than other games. Maybe the virtue and value of writing poetry, fiction, nonfiction, and of all the other arts as well, is that they channel the energies of certain clever people into ends other than destruction and death. In wars—and particularly in General Kelly's "modern warfare," in which clever technology plays such a chilling role, both on the battlefield and in the media packaging—one sees clearly how destructive a thing cleverness (intelligence?) can be, how deadly. If all good writers were not writers but scientists, they could likely devise more refinements for the death machine. As it is, perhaps, they do something that is relatively harmless. The more I spend my life trying to inflict as little damage as possible, I argue with myself, the better my life may be.

This argument assumes that *art does no damage*—or at least that art is incapable of doing as much damage as, say, science. My own experience tells me otherwise. Bad art, like bad science, has the power to have bad effects. Is it too much to hope, then, that good art can have good effects, however modest? My instincts say that is not too much to hope; but I cannot trust my "instincts," which may not be "instincts" at all but social constructs masquerading as instincts. These questions remind me insistently of my dream—of lying dead or dying facedown on a sofa, filled with numb confusion, detachment, futility, while killing goes on in the next room. How is it possible to construct a clear argument to guide me in my thinking beyond the impasse my dream—not to say reality—continues to project?

Perhaps I can begin with the fundamental error of the passage I wrote on January 16, which I take to be encapsulated in the following sentence: *There is a complete breakdown of conscience.* Having come to understand the concept of *conscience* in a special sense, I recognize in retrospect that my assumption that the war's outbreak represented a breakdown of conscience did violence to my convictions. The problem was not that conscience had broken down; the problem was that a conscience that could include the situation the world was facing on January 16 *had not yet been created.*

The top half of the frontispiece of the first edition of Thomas Hobbes's *Leviathan* shows a monstrous but beatific-faced monarch, holding a sword and scepter, looming over a pastoral countryside; in the foreground, an ordered city begins. The most striking feature of this image of kingship is the fact that the king's body is not shown in any recognizably realistic or quasi-anatomical fleshliness; instead, it is incorporated of many tiny human figures, all arranged harmoniously, like a chorus, and all turned to gaze on the king's Christlike face. The viewer sees everyone comprising the king's arms in left or right profile; all the figures in the king's torso have their backs rudely turned toward the audience. In effect, the monarch appears to be covered by a swarm of bees (or, as Christopher Pye describes it [296], a coat of mail), which on closer inspection turns out to consist of homunculi.

This image is a representation not of a mere fantasy but of the English Renaissance's concept of the body politic, which had a very definite anatomy in the literature, politics, and general mythology of that time and place. The morphology of the body politic is perhaps best described in Ernst H. Kantorowicz's remarkable book *The King's Two Bodies: A Study in Mediaeval Political Theology*, wherein Kantorowicz analyzes what he calls the "mystic fiction of the 'King's Two Bodies,'" as divulged by English jurists of the Tudor period and the times thereafter" (3). Kantorowicz finds "the first clear elaboration of that mystical talk" in Edmund Plowden's *Reports*, "collected and written under Queen Elizabeth," wherein Plowden writes that

[T]he King has in him two Bodies, *viz.*, a Body natural, and a Body politic. His Body natural (if it be considered in itself) is a Body mortal, subject to all Infirmities that come by Nature or Accident, to the Imbecility of Infancy or old Age, and to the like Defects that happen to the natural Bodies of other People. But his Body politic is a Body that cannot be seen or handled, consisting of Policy and Government . . . and the Body politic includes the Body natural, but the Body natural is the lesser, and with this the Body politic is consolidated . . . and these two Bodies are incorporated in one Person, and make one Body and not divers. (7, 9)

Though Kantorowicz's study is many-faceted, perhaps its most surprising feature, at least to nonexperts such as myself, is how thoroughly embedded, and how concretely embodied, is this "mystical fiction" in Tudor law. We would not be surprised to find such images and concepts in poetry, drama (the two-bodied monarch is a frequent governing structure in Shakespeare), paintings, theology, or political rhetoric; but the degree to which it permeated Tudor jurisprudence, as Kantorowicz presents it, is one of those elaborate surprises in which the Renaissance abounds. Courts argued, with deep seriousness, such issues as whether a given plot of land belonged to the monarch's "Body natural" (in which case it passed to his natural heirs after death) or to his "Body politic" (in which case it still belonged to the monarch after the death of the personal body, since the monarch in the "Body politic" was to all intents and purposes immortal). One striking example from *The King's Two Bodies* conveys this complicated, balanced strangeness with particular force. After many quotations from Plowden and elsewhere demonstrating the mystical unity of the king's "Body natural" and "the Body politic," Kantorowicz tells us,

Regardless of the dogmatic unity of the two bodies, a separation of one from the other was nevertheless possible, to wit, that separation which, with regard to the common man, is usually called Death. . . . [In the case *Hales v. Petit*] the court . . . was concerned with the legal consequences of a suicide, which the judges tried to define as an act of "Felony." Lord Dyer, Chief Justice, pointed out that suicide was a threefold crime. It was an offense against Nature, since it was contrary to the law of self-preservation; it was an offense against God as a violation of the sixth commandment; finally it was a crime committed "against the King in that hereby he has lost a Subject, and (as Brown termed it) he being the Head has lost one of his mystic Members." (12–15)

It's entertaining to imagine the tenor of those legal proceedings— and to wonder how Clarence Darrow, Perry Mason, or the whiz kids of *L.A. Law* would have handled it. But within the (what seems to us) loony logic of the doctrine of the King's Two Bodies, surely the suicide is guilty as charged, as the left hand would be guilty of an especially absurd crime against nature, God, and the brain if it chose to cut itself off, assuming it could find the means. And for the suicide, thus found guilty, the only appropriate sentence therefore would be death.

The fiction of the King's Two Bodies implies that conscience inheres not in any particular body but in a larger body, a body politic. For most contemporary Westerners, I suspect, this connection is not obvious. R. G. Collingwood, writing an "update" of Hobbes (*The New Leviathan*) in 1942, makes conscience a purely individual affair, nothing more than a sense of obligation leading to the conviction of duty:

> "[C]onscience" is as nearly infallible as a reasonable man will expect; but what is the business it "infallibly" carries out?
>
> To tell me that I am under an obligation; *not to tell me what that obligation is.* (122)

Elsewhere, though, he describes what he calls "social consciousness," which is closer to what I am calling "conscience":

> Every community is a community because there is something that its members share; what the members of a society share is *social*

consciousness. . . . Social consciousness, like all forms of consciousness, is primarily a practical consciousness; not a "making up your
mind *that*" but a "making up your mind *to*." It is primarily not an
awareness of being a member in a society, but an act of deciding to
become a member and to go on being a member. (139)

Society in Collingwood sounds curiously like a men's club. While his
very rational and pragmatic description of "membership" may ac-
cord with the way most of us think, at least most of the time, it does
not do justice to the power of the phenomenon of embeddedness
in a social whole—or the helpless confusion any one of us may
feel when that social whole begins to do things we deplore or fail
to understand. Nor does Collingwood do justice to the inherent
metaphorical power of words he deploys: *consciousness, conscience,
member.*

What is the "body politic" exactly? Of what does it consist? How
is it formed? What are its inner processes, its anatomy, its biology,
its evolution *as a body*? Coming to grips with the mythology of conscience demands acceptance of the metaphor of the body politic as a
provisionally literal thing, and points toward the question: *What is
the flesh of the body politic?* And for present purposes, given this curious fusion of the literal and the nonliteral, the question can profitably be rephrased in this way: *What are the mythologies of flesh?*

> Flesh: the soft substance of an animal body; the whole substance
> of the body; in, or with reference to the Biblical phrase "a heart
> of flesh," i.e. a heart capable of feeling, as opposed to "a heart of
> stone"; in euphemistic phrases with reference to sexual intercourse;
> "to go after strange flesh," a Biblical expression referring to unnatu-
> ral crime; the visible surface of the body, with reference to its color
> or appearance; one's near kindred or descendents; "one flesh," said
> of a husband and wife to express the closeness of the relation cre-
> ated by marriage; that which has corporeal life, all animals and in
> narrower sense all mankind; the physical or material frame of man-
> kind; the body of Christ, regarded as spiritually "eaten" by believers;

also applied mystically to the bread in the sacrament of the Lord's Supper. (*The Oxford English Dictionary*)

Everyone knows what flesh is—or do we? Can anyone really say what is the flesh of the living body and where it comes from?
God breath. Earth. Star gas.

Whether you trace the origin of your own body's flesh back to the fiat whereby God created the universe—in the beginning was the Word—or down into the infrastructure of subatomic particles or the muck of the primordial swamp, sooner or later the bewilderment and the mysteriousness turn out to be equivalent, since they are, in any and every direction, absolute. And if the nature of the all-too-common flesh of your all-too-common body is such a mystery, what shall we do with this other, less tangible thing, the flesh of the body politic?

We commonly mean any one of a number of things when we say *conscience*:

1. A good angel and a bad angel constantly perched like a pair of metaphysical vultures or mythic bookends on our shoulders, involving us in an ancient argument.

2. An inner voice constantly saying *yea* or *nay*.

3. A psychic construct, distinct from id and ego, comprising an implacable knot of guilt.

4. The light of God in the heart.

5. The voice of Nature in the deep mind.

6. Reason.

7. Intuition.

8. Natural fellow feeling.

9. Common sense: something like the Old English *inwit*.

The word "conscience" comes from Latin, from the infinitive *sciere*, meaning *to know*, and the prefix *con*, meaning *with*. "Conscience," then, in its root form means something like *knowledge-with, together-knowledge*. This etymology teaches us that Western culture has considered conscience to be knowledge transcending any single knower, existing in some kind of *with*-ness.

But who is knowing what, with whom, and how? Each of the notions in the list above is based on a different set of assumptions, different terms. And since we are implicitly dealing with a question of consciousness, this observation leads us to still another question: *What is the relationship between conscience and consciousness?*

No accident, the similarity of the words, since they come from the same root: *science/knowledge: sciere/to know: scio/I know* (*scio* being the first person form of the infinitive). *Con-scio-ious*: conscious = the condition *I-know-with*. In *Leviathan*, Hobbes recognizes, and blurs, this connection:

> When two, or more men, know of one and the same fact, they are said to be CONSCIOUS of it one to another; which is as much as to know it together. And because such are fittest witnesses of the facts of one another, or of a third; it was, and ever will be reputed a very Evill act, for any man to speak against his *Conscience*; or to corrupt or force another so to do: Insomuch that the plea of Conscience, has been alwayes hearkened unto very diligently in all times. Afterwards, men made use of the same word metaphorically, for the knowledge of their own secret facts, and secret thoughts; and therefore it is Rhetorically said, that the Conscience is a thousand witnesses. And last of all, men, vehemently in love with their own new opinions, (though never so absurd,) and obstinately bent to maintain them, gave those their opinions also that reverenced name of Conscience, as if they would have it seem unlawfull, to change or speak against them; and so pretend to know they are true, when they know at most, but that they think so. (131–32)

In a very different tone, Collingwood blurs this connection as well:

> How does a man become possessed of a social consciousness? How does he become able to think: "We will"?
>
> By the same process which enables him to think: "I will." (149)

First, there is the fiction of selfhood we gather together every morning of the world, out of the chaotic stuff of the mind asleep, and give the name "I." To be conscious, the word implies, is to enter a state of awareness that other minds ostensibly are able to share (regardless of whether they actually do so). To wake up in the morning, to open one's eyes and be conscious, is to become aware of one's bedroom in a way that another person, if he or she were present and also conscious, would also be aware of it. To become "conscious" of a flower on the wallpaper is to see it, to register it mentally, in the same way another "conscious" human being would do—"to be CONSCIOUS of it one to another," as Hobbes says. To become "conscious" of a memory that has previously been forgotten or repressed is to bring it into the same light—as the significant cliché has it—in which another "conscious" mind would hold a similar image, and to make that memory potentially (though perhaps not yet actually) communicable. Even to wake and recall a dream is to recall what any mind might recall if it were in my circumstances, working with my data. The *I-know-with* is the condition in which we implicitly say to our fellow human beings, "I am one of you, I am here in the world with you, knowing what you know, or what you would know or could know if you were seeing things from the same place, the same angle, from which I see them." This is a definition of consciousness suggested by the foundation of the word itself: Each of us alone is knowing what every other mind might know, and is knowing in the same way every other mind might know.

Conscience is harder to pin down. But one thing is immediately clear: The existence of conscience, the word's root signals, does not require an "I" to do the knowing-with. The word implies that the body of knowledge—the flesh of knowledge that the mythology of conscience demands—exists somewhere, somehow, outside what we regard as individual consciousness, because it excludes the "I."

Religions accept the idea that conscience is a "knowing-with-gods-or-God" and insist that its operation either is mediated by a religious organization (the temple at Delphi, the Catholic confessional) or is mystical (God's voice speaking in the inmost heart, as

Protestantism maintains). Either way, the "knowledge" exists without any necessity for a particular individual "I."

So: To be possessed by conscience is to know with God? But if there is knowledge-with-God, shouldn't I know God-things?

My response to this proposition is that of a radical agnostic: You can't convince me, with total certainty, that I know God-things.

> To make Covenant with God, is impossible, but by Mediation of such as God speaketh to, either by Revelation supernaturall, or by his Lieutenants that govern under him, and in his Name: For otherwise we know not whether our Covenants be accepted, or not.
> (Hobbes 197)

Other possibilities, then: Where else might this knowledge that is conscience be hiding?

Nature? Does knowing-with-nature exist? But if it exists, shouldn't we all know nature-things: hawk-things, tree-things? Obviously, such propositions are arguable; but again, you can't convince me that I know these things.

> To make Covenant with bruit Beasts, is impossible; because not understanding our speech, they understand not, nor accept of any translation of Right; nor can translate any Right to another: and without mutuall acceptation, there is no Covenant. (Hobbes 197)

Then maybe conscience, like consciousness, means "knowledge-with-humanity" but transcending any individual human "I":

a. Via authority, embodied externally in the mortmain of tradition and the law and/or internally in the superego.

b. Via empathy, an emotional attachment to the understanding that other individuals must be as we are and must suffer as we suffer.

c. Via imagination, which gives us the capacity to have the illusion of accurate knowing, as in b above.

d. Via biology, through the DNA of the literal flesh—as the conscience of bees and ants must be operative, making them the only creatures other than human beings capable of waging war.

e. Or even: Via language (inclusive of all the above).

In our separate consciousnesses we experience ourselves as isolated from each other and are likewise or therefore isolated from any of these sources of conscience. As far as any one among us can demonstrate, conscience is a fiction—and a fallible fiction, necessarily—whether it be posited on God or gods or hawks or trees or (especially) communally accumulated experience or the capacity for utterance or the mysterious common flesh of humankind.

Consider the following parable:

In a world not ours, an ideal conscience exists. I am postulating a science-fiction order in which all human beings are linked by a perfect telepathy, a perfect together-knowledge. In that world, there can be no wrongdoing because there can be no hiding, no lying, no subterfuge, no disguise, since the thoughts of every individual are instantly known by everyone. In that world human violence does not exist because the pain inflicted by one person upon another will be felt instantly not only by the victim but also by the perpetrator *and* by every other consciousness. In short, consciousness and conscience are not separated: in that ideal world, the two words are made one. In that world every person is bound in the flesh of a single "body"—an objectively operating body politic—within which the operation of conscience can only be perfect, complete, and overwhelming.

If such a conscience suddenly descended upon us in a shower of gold, the whole structure of human life would alter completely, all at a stroke. The arrival of such a conscience would, by fiat, implement the perfect revolution. All the institutions of separation and domination would vanish in a microsecond. Government would transmute into the perfect democracy, the perfect socialism: government would, in fact, become perfectly unnecessary. Conscience would be government, religion, education, all bound in an immanent knowledge, inseparable from consciousness. Whitman successfully conjured this world in "Song of Myself": conscience, fait accompli.

In this nonexistent place and time, every human works as hard as necessary, for instance, to grow food to stop the gnaw of hunger in every human belly on earth, because the hunger of a single man, woman, or child anywhere is the hunger of every single man, woman, and child everywhere. Every feature of society would be instantaneously, spontaneously redesigned for one purpose and one purpose only: the perfect elimination of pain.

Conscience is the true name of Utopia.

That such a world would be unbearable is obvious—because, made by and held within the world that has so created us, we are too weak to bear what in the name of any moral logic we ought to bear. In this perfect, overwhelming conscience, all the suffering the world imposes, beyond the control of even the most perfect human organization, would be transmitted inescapably to everyone. This would be the genie's curse, the dark side of the good wish. The sum of every hangnail, every toothache, every hunger, every cancer, every accident, every pang of guilt—even what might well be the devastating intensity of collective joy—would impinge constantly and unconditionally on us all.

In the abstract, that conscience would be perfect: a universe of redistributed pain. But in the concrete, who among us could bear it? Or who among us would *want* it, since it would be, in some ways, the perfect totalitarian state? Its motto would be *Conscience: Live it or leave it*. And there would be only one ticket out, which no one would be able to take because every loss of a member would be unbearable to all the others.

Describing the practical incommunicability of pain, Elaine Scarry observes that

it often happens that two people can be in a room together, the one in pain, the other either partially or wholly unaware of the first person's pain. But the implicit question that is being asked here, "How is it that one person can be in the presence of another person in pain and not know it?," leads inevitably to a second question . . . "How is it that one person can be in the presence of another person in pain and not know it—not know it to the point where he himself inflicts it, and goes on inflicting it?" (12)

Hobbes is notorious for insisting on such perverse but accurate reversals of certain "intuitive" truths, the binding of torturer and tortured, of aggressor and the victim of aggression:

> To have done more hurt to a man, than he can, or is willing to expiate, *enclineth the doer to hate the sufferer*. For he must expect revenge, or forgivenesse; both which are hatefull. (163, italics added)

Just as we tell ourselves in all our culture-myths that we are bound to each other by love and selflessness, we often appear to demonstrate by the substance of our lives that we are bound preeminently in willful ignorance and hate.

Both mind and literal flesh are arguably an evolutionary product of aggression. The biologist Lynn Margulis, speculating on ways single-celled creatures may have begun to build themselves into multicellular bodies, hypothesizes

> that all . . . phenomena of mind, from perception to consciousness [and presumably also conscience], originated from an unholy microscopic alliance between hungry killer bacteria and their potential archaebacterial victims. The hungry killers were extraordinarily fast-swimming, skinny bacteria called spirochetes. . . . The fatter, slow-moving potential victims, the second kind of bacteria called archaebacteria, were quite different from the spirochetes. By resisting death the archaebacteria incorporated their would-be, fast-moving killers into their bodies. The archaebacteria survived, continuing to be infected by the spirochetes. The odd couple lived together; the archaebacteria were changed, but not killed, by their attackers; the victims did not entirely succumb. . . . Our cells, including our nerve

cells, may be products of such mergers—the thin, transparent bodies of the spirochete enemies sneakily incorporated inextricably and forever. . . . Cultural analogues of such mergers exist. . . . Speculation, I claim, is legacy of the itching enmities of unsteady truce. Speculation is the mutual stimulation of the restrained microbial inhabitants that, entirely inside their former archaebacterial enemies, have strongly interacted with them for hundreds of millions of years. Our nerve cells are the outcome of an ancient, nearly immortal marriage of two archenemies who have managed to coexist: the former spirochetes and former archaebacteria that now comprise our brains. (161–63)

This myth ("hypothesis," "speculation") of bio-creation has many ramifications; here one may find the paradigm for, well, everything: egg and sperm, male and female, predator and prey, war, flesh, dialectics, the human world we know and the love we love it with. In this scenario, body and body politic are founded on ur-aggression. But if, as the old song says, that's all there is, and if Elaine Scarry is also right to say that "pain . . . centrally entail[s], require[s] . . . [the] shattering of language" (5), how can language be the binding force of the body politic? How do suffering and saying balance, reinforce, negate each other?

Perhaps we are divided by our natures, because by our natures we are too weak to be united. Or: we are too weak to be united by any forces other than dark, negative ones. We often appear united only by suspicion, greed, selfishness, and hatred—forces that make us *refuse* to acknowledge the suffering of others, and that translate themselves into such immediate and potentially negative "natural bonds" as those of blood and tribe pure and simple. Judged in these terms, no genuine conscience exists; no overarching connection exists. There is only the fiction of conscience, the ancient myth of connection: an assumption that if conscience didn't exist, its creation would be necessary; that our survival, weak as we individually are (unlike, for instance, rattlesnakes), dictates it. It is necessary to create—if only by imposition of myth—the interconnectedness that conscience implies. And if it is necessary to create conscience, the myth assumes, it must therefore be possible to do so.

Articles of Faith of the Mythology of Conscience:

1. If there is no body politic, it is necessary to create one.

2. The body politic must have flesh. (Flesh: *the whole substance of the body.*) So that

3. in creating the body politic, as in the creation of any body, we are involved in the creation of flesh.

The perfect conscience would be a perfect telepathy. And language is the fullest telepathy we have—imperfect, yes, but arguably our most immediate access to the reality of other people's pain. Conscience is the binding force of the body politic; language is the locus, the substance, the connective tissue of conscience. It follows, therefore, that language is the flesh of the body politic.

Conscience is a story, then? A fiction? Words?

But a fiction is at least a real fiction.

Suppose we were to attempt to project an image of the body politic of the United States of America in early 1991. What sort of image could crystallize us? We photograph (or film) ourselves as literal multitudes; we symbolize our unity (obsessively, from a British point of view) with flags and eagles. But we lack—and may experience nostalgia for, when we view a compact icon like the woodcut of the King's Two Bodies—a political myth that can find incisive expression in a single allegorical image. And if the English Renaissance exerts a powerful spell over us, draws us with a golden age's force field of desire, it is partly, I think, on account of its marvelous, bizarre complexity and partly on account of what we perceive as its clarity. No matter how one may feel about, for instance, the image of the King's Two Bodies that dominates the frontispiece of *Leviathan*

(I for one find it both powerful and repellant), one cannot deny that it is *clear*, literally and symbolically—a convincing representation of the body politic of that particular place and time.

Our sense of the coherence of the Renaissance political mythology is largely an illusion. Marie Axton maintains—in *The Queen's Two Bodies*, an amplification and in part a correction of Kantorowicz—that " 'The king's two bodies' was never a *fact*, nor did it ever attain the status of orthodoxy; it remained a controversial idea. The idea seemed, for a limited historical span, to express a precarious balance of power between the king and the state" (x). Axton also shows how this "controversial idea" was used for political manipulation. On the one hand, Elizabeth

> and her advisers made full use of an ideology which consisted of technical concepts, myth and metaphysics, suggestions, surmise, flattery and subtle coercion, to maintain a precarious balance of power. (145–46)

Meanwhile,

> Under Elizabeth the theory of the two bodies had been used to criticize and coerce the Queen. Elizabeth had suffered humiliations, had changed tactics without ever permitting Parliament a full and open debate on the succession. Outside Parliament she tolerated the fictions by which men of law pointed out the discrepancy between her two bodies and made artful criticisms of her policy. (146)

Historical facts, always more complicated and unsettled than we want them to be, prove repeatedly that myths, however united and uniting, can be used as weapons. But the *facts* of history never block the projection of our own longing, of our own lacking.

This process happens not because we don't have political mythology (far from it), nor because we are not a body politic. One point of American pride is that we have the historical assurance of knowing exactly when and where our social contract came into being; we have, as they say, the documents. Those documents, in fact, have a quasi-sacred stature for many Americans. However, that historical

assurance is the foundation of our mythos, and the actual beginning of the American body politic turns out to be untraceable. There
is no single crystallizing moment. The Declaration of Independence
is already the expression of a "people." And many historians argue
(as several did at the end of Ken Burns's 1990 PBS documentary
The Civil War) that 1861–65 is the defining period of our "national
unity."

What we feel, in the presence of that Renaissance monarchial
image, is a commensurate lack of coherence, which is both the gift
and the wound of our political experiment. Perhaps the most distinct feature of American political life is profound oscillation between experiencing the incoherence of our body politic *as* a gift and
experiencing it *as* a wound. Which image of ourselves do we choose
to project: loose collective of self-reliant individualists, or one nation
under God fused in the democratic melting pot? We shift with the
weight of events. In the post–World War II 1950s, we seem to have
needed homogeneity; and though there was plenty of dissent bub-
bling under the surface, not least in the gathering force of the civil
rights movement, many Americans would have been satisfied to be
part of a *corpus mysticum* with the vapid WASP face of Pat Boone.
Conversely, the most characteristic image of the 1960s might arguably be a photo of the multitude gathered before the stage at Wood-
stock. The difference between those two ideas is vast but quintessen-
tially American, comprising the monotonously individualistic on
the one hand and the facelessly multitudinous on the other—each
illusory, and each in its way exclusionary. If it were possible to make
a woodcut of that difference, it would do as a frontispiece for some
midcentury neo-Hobbes's *American Leviathan* (an idea that seems
not to have occurred to Charles and William Beard when they published a book by that name in 1930; their frontispiece, instead, is a
black-and-white photo of a small ship confronting an iceberg, cap-
tioned "A Coast Guard Vessel on Iceberg Patrol Discovers a Floating
Monster of the North in an Atlantic Sealane," a representation of
technological society's encounter with a leviathan of a most un-
Hobbesian kind).

Most of us would be at a loss to suggest a single image that would
even begin to summarize what we have been from 1968 to the
present—although I suspect that for better or worse, the war with
Iraq may already be providing a locus. Post-Vietnam America was
in a condition of serious demystification; whether you thought that
was a good thing depends on what your political convictions were.
Many citizens suffered incoherence-anxiety during those years; for
them, the fracturing of the 1950s illusion of American social and
political homogeneity was experienced as a wound, or as a disease
that George H. W. Bush called *Vietnam Syndrome,* for which he
hailed victory in Kuwait as a cure. The soldiers who carried out the
combat in the Gulf region were projected more as physicians and
medical technicians (albeit "heroic" ones) than as warriors; the media portrayal of the war smelled strongly of the operating room. A
heavy odor of antiseptic and anesthetic lingered in the air, and the
subject (whether patient or victim—and *was* the subject Kuwait, or
the United States? Who was the main beneficiary of this "healing"?)
was kept carefully under sterile wraps. Those of us in the spectator's
seats beyond the plate-glass arena window watched either with the
helpless grief of relatives of the stricken (What's the prognosis?
What will the specialists say?) or with the obsessive professional interest of the student surgeon (What happens next? Can I learn that
technique?).

Meanwhile, real doctors, responsible for the well-being of actual
individual bodies, had a different understanding of the war. Chris
Hedges, a journalist captured by the Iraqi army for a few days in the
aftermath of the conflict, gives this account:

> An [Iraqi] Army doctor, his eyes red and several days' growth of
> beard on his chin, sat in a small room in an army encampment.
> "We have destroyed Kuwait," said the doctor, who had lost his
> closest friend to an allied cluster bomb, "but the Americans have
> destroyed Iraq.
> "I do not defend this invasion of Kuwait, because I am a doctor

and I do not defend the taking of life," he went on. "But there is nothing left of my country. America has been very brutal." In Basra alone, the doctor estimated, more than 1,000 civilians had died in the allied bombing.

"Your great American soldiers can go home to their families now," he said. "They can tell them they devastated our lives and the lives of our children. Our country is no more." (14)

The tone of this statement contrasts tellingly with that of Lieut. Gen. Charles Horner, the commander of allied air forces in the Gulf; here he speaks with the pragmatic authority of a physician recounting particularly radical cancer surgery, in which the object of discussion is not the patient but the cancer:

> "We wanted to seize the initiative immediately," General Horner said. "In the first 10 minutes of the war, we wanted to shock him and paralyze him.
>
> "We flew as many combat missions in one day as he experienced in eight years of war with Iran," the general added, referring to the Iraqi military. (Schmitt 16)

Of course, the second paragraph makes the literal context of the remarks abundantly clear; but the syntax is sufficiently skewed that the reporter finds it necessary to clarify (arguably inaccurately) the referent of the singular masculine pronoun.

It is traditional to refer to an enemy nation with a collective "he," but the desire to make the war with Iraq a war against Saddam Hussein was, as everyone noticed, a matter of special urgency in the first Bush administration. Reporters said that Bush wanted to "personalize" the war; it appears more accurate to say that Bush understood (whether consciously or unconsciously) that to dignify Hussein as a double-bodied Leviathan would be to blur the issue of whose bodies were being bombed. "We have no quarrel with the Iraqi people," Bush said repeatedly; "our quarrel is with their leader." Yet at the end of the hostilities, it was quite apparent who was alive and who was not—and as I write it remains unclear whether a defeated Iraq with Hussein at its "head" is not more politically advantageous for the United States than the alternative. We have seen few images of the 100,000 or so Iraqi soldiers who reportedly died in Kuwait; we have no idea how many civilians perished ("In Basra alone, the doctor estimated, more than 1,000 civilians had died"). Bush was caught in a double bind here: To target Hussein for assassination in the "Body natural" would have been illegal (if not, perhaps more tellingly, impossible to carry through); to unleash the most deadly nonnuclear arsenal the world has ever assembled on a relatively helpless population and on an exhausted army might have been viewed as immoral, had there been no mediating rhetoric. But to wipe out the "mystic Members" of a two-bodied king was a strategy so rhetorically ambiguous that no one could sort out the terms of it until the war was a *fait accompli*.

As for the *corpus mysticum* of the United States in the course of the war, it came to look increasingly robotic. In spite of General Schwartzkopf's avuncular disavowals of a "Nintendo war," clearly our machinery fought the most, and Iraq and Kuwait looked increasingly like laboratories for test runs of the latest equipment. One reporter writes,

> Since the fighting with Iraq ended, top Air Force commanders have been studying the details of the air campaign—the most intensive ever waged—to draw lessons for future conflicts. . . .
>
> Lieut. Gen. Charles Horner, the commander of allied air forces in the gulf, said in an interview that the war had established that radar-evading "stealth" technology and the pinpoint accuracy of precision-guided bombs were changing the nature of air warfare. For instance, the stealthy F-117, using guided bombs, accounted for only 3 percent of allied aircraft but struck 43 percent of the Iraqi targets that were hit, Air Force officials said. (Schmitt 1, 16)

This account renders the dead (American and Iraqi alike), and those who killed them, invisible. Such rhetoric is a constant in accounts of war; Elaine Scarry describes how

the written and spoken record of war over many centuries certifies
the ease with which human powers of description break down in
the presence of battle, the speed with which they back away from
injuring and begin to take as their subject the most incidental or
remote activities occuring there, rather than holding onto what is
everywhere occurring at its center and periphery. The enumeration
of the paths by which injuring disappears from view only begins
with the one already named here: omission. (66)

New in the present instance is how much America as a body begins
to look suspiciously like Robocop: shiny, faceless, urgent, sincere in
its desire to follow its prime directives. And, like a stealth bomber, it
is a machine that is purposely made difficult to see.

Though new in form, this image is remarkably Hobbesian in
spirit. The introduction to *Leviathan* begins with the following
passage:

Nature (the Art whereby God hath made and governes the World) is
by the *Art* of man, as in many other things, so in this also imitated,
that it can make an Artificial Animal. For seeing life is but a motion
of Limbs, the beginning whereof is in some principall part within;
why may we not say, that all *Automata* (Engines that move themselves by springs and wheeles as doth a watch) have an artificiall
life? For what is the *Heart*, but a *Spring*; and the *Nerves*, but so
many *Strings*; and the *Joynts*, but so many *Wheeles*, giving motion
to the whole Body, such as was intended by the Artificer? *Art* goes
yet further, imitating that Rationall and most excellent worke of
Nature, *Man*. For by Art is created that great LEVIATHAN called a
COMMON-WEALTH. (81)

Hobbes wonderfully (and, from our perspective, maybe a bit
quaintly) blurs the boundaries between art, science, and religion to
produce the conceit out of which the whole argument of *Leviathan*
springs. It is far more bourgeois than the *corpus mysticum* of Plowden's double-bodied king ("Of course," Kantorowicz tells us [12],
"that metaphor was very old"); it looks forward to the industrial revo-

lution rather than backward toward feudalism and the hegemony of the Catholic Church. Being, for Hobbes, postlapsarian—coming after the "Fall" of the English Civil War, while Plowden's mystical "Body politic" comes before—this clockwork Leviathan is both serious and silly. And it is palpably, self-consciously, a fiction.

The Robo-nation image projected by the Bush administration, the military, and the press is a less conscious fiction than Hobbes's, and is infinitely less witty—but it is nonetheless a fiction, through which various realities keep trying to break (as the Iraqi doctor quoted above demonstrates). How much reality erupts into this nation's public consciousness will depend partly on the press's determination to reveal it, partly on the government's determination to conceal or skew it, and partly on the public's willingness to receive it. My suspicion, and my fear, is that the majority of Americans will embrace the clean, inhuman projection of a body politic that this war and its aftermath are in the process of producing. The desire for coherence, for compact summing-up, is difficult to resist.

But resistance is clearly called for. If the aura of the war with Iraq is in part the consequence of what might be called bad art, then the only antidote for it is good art. Artists—no less than presidents, dictators, generals, censors, journalists, public relations firms, and the "authorization" of private citizens—have a role in creating the body politic. In fact, if there is any truth to the notion that language is the flesh of the body politic, then writers bear an unusually significant responsibility for the composition, and the healthy revision, of that flesh. Our particular moment makes the task difficult because the issues are nebulous, slippery, incoherent.

But perhaps it is that very incoherence that we need to learn to embrace.

Leviathan describes the genesis of the curious two-bodied monarch Kantorowicz described. That creature is born when a mass of individuals

appoint[s] one man, or Assembly of men, to beare their Person; and
every one to owne, and acknowledge himself to be Author of whatsoever he that so beareth their Person, shall Act, or cause to be
Acted, in those things which concern the Common Peace and
Saftie; and therein to submit their Wills, every one to his Will, and
their Judgments, to his Judgment. This is more than Consent, or
Concord; it is a real Unity of them all, in one and the same Person,
made by Covenant of every man and with every man, in such a
manner, as if every man should say to every man, I *Authorize and
give up my Right of Governing my selfe, to this Man, or this Assembly
of men, on this condition, that thou give up thy Right to him, and Autho-
rise all his Actions in like manner*. This done, the Multitude so united
in one Person, is called a COMMON-WEALTH, in latine CIVITAS.
This is the generation of that great LEVIATHAN, or rather (to speak
more reverently) of that *Mortall God*, to which we owe under the
Immortall God, our peace and deference. For by this Authoritie,
given him by every particular man in the Common-Wealth, he hath
the use of so much Power and Strength conferred on him, that by
terror thereof, he is inabled to forme the wills of them all, to Peace
at home, and mutuall ayd against their enemies abroad. (227–28)

This description ironically plays off the myth of the genesis of the
god-king; but it infuses that older notion with a new myth of the formation of the body politic, which is, I am arguing, the locus of what
we call conscience. It is formed, in Hobbes's description, by a kind
of unspoken speech—"as if every man should say to every man, I
Authorize"—and is consensus operating beyond the will of any particular person: "This is more than Consent, or Concord; it is a real
Unity of them all, in one and the same Person, made by Covenant of
every man and with every man. . . ." The body politic is that covenant
whereby these people know together who and what they collectively
are. Hobbes's metaphorical saying of human to human, this covenant as if of speech, is for him the basis of a nation, whose body is
the body politic and whose soul is the *Zeitgeist*.

Christopher Pye argues that "Hobbes's insistence" at this point in the text "confirms Ernst Kantorowicz's observation that in Renaissance theories of sovereignty the king's artificial, metaphoric Body Politic was seen to represent his most authentic presence" (284), and no doubt this is true. However, since the "mystical doctrine" of the king's two bodies is by definition precisely double, there is another message, not contradicting Pye's: the implication that the king's "authentic presence" is an *effect* of the people's metaphoric speech. This is not an idea that Hobbes chose to emphasize, partly because he was intent on making an airtight argument in favor of sovereign government and against civil disobedience; he himself was, paradoxically enough, a bourgeois royalist, an egalitarian antidemocrat. Hobbes's fantasy of humanity's original condition admits of

> no Culture of the Earth; no Navigation, nor use of the commodities that may be imported by Sea; no commodious Building; no Instruments of moving, and removing such things as require much force; no Knowledge of the face of the Earth; no account of Time; no Arts; no Letters; no Society; and which is worst of all, continuall feare, and danger of violent death; And the life of man, solitary, poore, nasty, brutish, and short. (186)

This is a "hypothetical condition," C. B. Macpherson says, that would "exist if there were no common power able to restrain individuals, no law and no law-enforcement," rhetorically designed "to demonstrate, to men who could follow Hobbes in 'this Inference, made from the Passions,' that they should, in their own interests as civilized men, do whatever was necessary to avoid getting into this state of nature or anything like it" (40–41). Hobbes's state of nature is balanced only by the "as if" that "authorizes" the Leviathan of the commonwealth, an uttering-forth as mystical and ultimately unexaminable as the Word that utters forth the world in the Gospel of John. The social contract stands between civilized humanity and the state of nature like a mirror image of the swords of flame held up by the angels, forcing Adam and Eve to keep their backs to Eden; and like those cosmos-dividing swords, it is nowhere to be found, by archaeologists, historians, or anthropologists. The social contract, as Hobbes describes it, remains incorrigibly metaphorical and covertly mythic.

Reading Hobbes is interesting and rewarding for many reasons, including the tension between science and mythology that breathes in every sentence of *Leviathan*. Of the depth of this struggle, Hobbes himself appears both aware and unaware. Macpherson convincingly discusses the conscious and the unconscious bourgeois and anti-bourgeois character of Hobbes's project (51–60); doubtless someone else has somewhere fully explored his anti-Christian Christianity and his scientific antiempiricism. One can bridge the gap between Hobbes's state of nature and his political state using any of these tensions; the true basis of the "as if" that conjures the Leviathan of the body politic can be viewed as mystical if you like, or statistical if you don't. But my purpose here is to put forward a different hypothetical bridge, to shift the terms at least provisionally, proposing not mythic or religious or sociological apologetics for the Leviathan or its contemporary equivalent, but rather aesthetic ones. I propose to view the creation of the body politic as collective aesthetic activity.

The example of the opening of *Leviathan* teaches us that the body politic need not be conceived of as a human. Hobbes envisions it as made in the *image* of a man, but that vision differs from the figure on his book's frontispiece, which *is* a man, albeit an extraordinary one. If not a human, then why even the *image* of a human? Is the shape of the human body anything like the shape of the cells that compose it? Why then should we have the hubris to assume that the whole of which each of us is somehow a part bears any resemblance to our body? To assume that it can only be so is a failure of the imagination.

In *Twilight of the Idols*, Nietzsche writes,

[O]ne belongs to the whole, one is in the whole; there is nothing which could judge, measure, compare, or sentence our being, for that would mean judging, measuring, comparing, or sentencing the whole. But there is nothing besides the whole. That nobody is held responsible any longer, that the mode of being may not be traced back to a *causa prima*, that the world does not form a unity either as a sensorium or as "spirit"—that alone is the great liberation; with this alone is the innocence of becoming restored. (501)

Nietzsche has conceived an intersubjectivity of being that is, at least from our perspective, unfathomably formless; typically, he rejoices fiercely in being freed from bondage to any graven image. We are not made in the image of God; the whole is not made in the image of a man: it is neither "sensorium" nor "spirit." Foucault describes the dark side of this shapeless wholeness; in such a structure, he tells us,

Power relations are both intentional and nonsubjective. If in fact they are intelligible, this is not because they are the effect of another instance that "explains" them, but rather because they are imbued, through and through, with calculation: there is no power that is exercised without a series of aims and objectives. But this does not mean that it results from the choice or decision of an individual subject; let us not look for the headquarters that presides over its rationality; neither the caste which governs, nor the groups which control the state apparatus, nor those who make the most important economic decisions direct the entire network of power that functions in a society (and makes *it* function); the rationality of power is characterized by tactics that are quite often explicit at the restricted level where they are inscribed (the local cynicism of power). . . . [T]he logic is perfectly clear, the aims decipherable, and yet it is often the case that no one is there to have invented them, and few who can be said to have formulated them: an implicit characteristic of the great anonymous, almost unspoken strategies which coordinate the loquacious tactics whose "inventors" or decisionmakers are often without hypocrisy. (94–95)

While for Nietzsche "wholeness" is a boundless field for the un-bridled activity of the naked will, Foucault depicts the wholeness of the state as a science fiction creature, all transparent protoplasm and veins of arcing blue light. The organism possesses a superabun-dance of nerves but is brainless, not requiring a brain to contain whatever thoughts it may or may not think; thus decentered, it is safe from assault, and inscrutable. These are not pleasing or com-forting images. Either may be close to the truth; or neither may be more real than Hobbes's clockwork Leviathan. Collectively, these three images form a useful counterweight to the monolithic bionic depiction of nationality currently being assembled in the crucibles and silicon valleys of the White House. But—and this is the crucial point—they are *all fictions*. No one of them has any exclusive claim on the individual or collective imagination.

Much of the enormous amount of discussion generated by the war with Iraq—among politicians, newscasters, "experts" of various per-suasions, and people on the street—has strained to find a convinc-ing analogy for the present situation. The two most obvious depict the Gulf conflict as similar to World War II or the conflict in Viet-nam, and the opposed values of these images are obvious. As pro-test against and support for the Iraq war mounted during its first few days, these two allegorical representations found their way onto the street. Marchers on either side of the issue carried signs depict-ing Saddam Hussein as a non-Aryan Hitler and George H. W. Bush as a yuppie Nixon. The familiar chants "Hell no we won't go" and "Love it or leave it" echoed across the Mall in Washington, D.C. All of us who remember the 1960s experienced a powerful déjà vu in the first few days of the war—all the familiar gestures, slogans, and symbols returned in a rush.

Then the dissident side of that rush faded: partly because the media stopped covering it (as enthusiasm for the war grew, journal-ists seemed more and more inclined to give space to only one kind of "patriotism"), and partly because uncertainty mounted among dissidents—not of their convictions but of the terms in which they could convincingly express them. The Bush administration was ready with means to co-opt the protest. ("I feel guilty," a San Francisco poet said to me, "but I don't go to protest marches because I'm convinced that's *exactly what the government expects me to do*"; Frederic Jameson articulates a similar sentiment, virtually prophesying the present situation, when he describes how resistance in a "postmodern" world is "all somehow secretly disarmed and reabsorbed by a system of which [resisters] might well be considered a part, since they can achieve no distance from it" [49].) But Kuwait is *not* Vietnam, any more than Iraq is Nazi Germany. The breakdown in the momentum of public protest likely came about because those who would dissent were seeking sincere and effective means to protest what was happening in a present unfolding at spectacular speed, and not what happened twenty years ago. Meanwhile, Bush shamelessly deployed the rhetoric of World War II—this was a "just war," we were told; this was a war that pitted "good against evil"; the United States was "on God's side" and doing "the hard work of freedom"—and if the public opinion polls can be believed, his rhetorical strategy, however transparent, worked.

If language truly is the flesh of the body politic, it is very insensitive flesh, containing few nerves, few ganglia. Or, put another way: Language is very weak telepathy.

For this reason, I was certainly wrong to write, on January 16, "There is a complete breakdown of conscience." I should have said, "The conscience that will connect me with these events—the knowledge that will bring these events and my mind together—that fiction has not yet been created."

It is necessary (now, always, forever) to create that conscience, and for better or worse *it will be created*—it will arise inevitably out of what we all do and say and think. In the present instance, when it arises it will be Bush's obsessively reiterated "new world order." Conscience is a collective work of art. Its form is not predetermined;

its nature is not fixed; it is never finished, but at some point—as Flaubert observed about novels—it is abandoned.

Near the beginning of Joyce's *Portrait of the Artist as a Young Man*, Stephen Dedalus, a schoolboy studying geography, indulges in a bit of instinctive self-definition, exactly the sort of thing most of us can remember doing as children:

> He opened the geography to study the lesson; but he could not learn the names of places in America. Still they were all different places that had those different names. They were all in different countries and the countries were in continents and the continents were in the world and the world was in the universe.
>
> He turned to the flyleaf of the geography and read what he had written there: himself, his name and where he was.
>
>
> Stephen Dedalus
> Class of Elements
> Clongowes Wood College
> Sallins
> County Kildare
> Ireland
> Europe
> The World
> The Universe
>
>
> That was in his writing: and Fleming one night for a cod had written on the opposite page:
>
>
> Stephen Dedalus is my name,
> Ireland is my nation.
> Clongowes is my dwellingplace
> And heaven my destination. (15–16)
>

Stephen is attempting to place himself in the universe he knows, within all those mysterious places that have names—and in that se-

ries the world and the universe seem no more far away and mysterious than the place names of distant America. Joyce allows Stephen's
meditation to leap immediately from his list of environments to
a poem, as if the poem were a crystallization of his thinking. The
poem, of course, is not Stephen's own composition—it is simply
there; it confronts him. Despite the important fact that it pretends to
speak to him in his own voice, out of his own deepest self, it is written by someone else in a handwriting other than his own, put in his
book "for a cod." But it suddenly does not *seem* a joke. It assumes a
cold significance in the context of this very serious act of contemplation. This text is, in its way, omniscient; it wants to describe existence
as a sort of square (or perhaps a rectangle like a coffin), one boundary of which is stated in each of its four lines. The poem assumes for
Stephen at this moment a mighty authority. The last line especially,
which signifies the ultimate limit of the self, is deeply serious.

The poem offers no solutions. It answers no questions and it
gives no advice. If anything, it makes Stephen's bewilderment loom
larger, appearing as it does in the impersonal guise of an oracular
restatement of the problem *I am I, I exist in this place, and I will die.*
The poem focuses Stephen's thinking. After he has read it once,
Joyce tells us, "He read the verses backward but then they were not
poetry. Then he read the flyleaf from the bottom to the top till he
came to his own name. That was he: and he read down the page
again" (16).

Joyce gives us an important clue as to why the poem has an impact on Stephen different from the impact of the list of facts: *the
poem cannot be read backward.* The order of the list of facts allows it
to be comprehended as a *list* read in either direction, as a perception
of the ordering of things from the self radiating out to that impersonal abstraction "The Universe," or just as easily vice versa, from
the godlike impersonal down to the mote of self. The poem permits
of no such reversal. Its structure carries the reader in one direction
only, precisely as time does: from the self out toward the final limit
of the self. The poem centers Stephen in a way the list does not. It

gives a human ordering of thought to a group of otherwise inhuman circumstances.

In all this thinking, Stephen is portrayed as feeling distinctly uncomfortable. He is facing "big questions" and doing so in a serious way. He is confronted by two modes of information: the list's piling up of facts, and the poem. Both are tools, modes of discovery. Each helps him to identify himself and his situation in the world. Neither clarifies the mystery of his existence; each serves, in its own way, to make him more aware of what he *cannot* know. At this point, Stephen makes a leap into ultimate questioning:

> What was after the universe? Nothing. But was there anything round the universe to show where it stopped before the nothing began? It could not be a wall but there could be a thin thin line there all around everything. Only God could do that. He tried to think what a big thought that must be but he could only think of God. God was God's name just as his name was Stephen. *Dieu* was French for God and that was God's name too; and when anyone prayed to God and said *Dieu* then God knew at once that it was a French person that was praying. But though there were different names for God in all the different languages in the world and God understood what all the people who prayed said in their different languages still God remained always the same God and God's real name was God. (16)

Led relentlessly on in his questioning from the perceived and imagined facts to poetry to theology, Stephen comes to consider (however confusedly) the nature of language itself, how it allows us to think certain things and prevents us from thinking others. When he reaches this part of his meditation, Stephen (who is getting tired by now) abruptly falls back into a habitual pattern. Up to this point, he has revealed his kinship with all human beings in his lostness in the universe; in the end, however, he falls back into being limited to his language group, into chauvinism, a dyed-in-the-wool speaker of English: "and God's real name was God." Not *Dieu*: God.

We can easily forgive Stephen for his lapse. He is only a child, after all, and he has worn himself out thinking these "big thoughts." "It made him very tired to think that way," Joyce tells us. "It made him feel his head very big" (16). Furthermore, Stephen is human; we all behave this way. When questions become too large for us, we tend to fall back on what we have inherited in the way of answers, on our unexamined assumptions. In this sense, the national in us— Irish or Chinese or American—is the worst in us, the unthinking nationalism that turns flesh against flesh, divides the world into *us* and *them*, makes wars between those who say *God* and those who say *Dieu*, often for no better reason than that simple fact.

While we can and should forgive Stephen, we cannot and should not forgive the poem. The poem has failed Stephen. It has authoritatively professed to be something it is not, claiming to be both all-inclusive and personal. Speaking in the guise of a voice from Stephen's own deep mind, even appropriating his name, it has drawn a "thin thin line" around his entire existence, pretending to comprehend it. The ersatz nature of this omniscience reveals itself in Stephen's spin-off train of contemplation. The poem is omniscient, yes, but it knows nothing. It is too monolithic; it is, strange to say, too *clear*. When Stephen falls back as he must on life in the human world—and on the politics of language—the poem does not help him. The poem has nothing to say about these matters; and Stephen, unequipped, founders. The poem has propelled him into territory where he is unprepared to go, and then abandoned him. It is culpable; it bears part of the responsibility for his failure, for the dangerous ugliness of his one political thought. It has authorized a false idea of conscience.

Of course, the poem is not much of a poem. Perhaps that is the problem. Or maybe the problem is in even the hint of the expectation that a poem ought to be useful; perhaps that expectation turns us into Nietzsche's Socrates, who could comprehend only one kind of poetry.

the *Aesopian fable*; and this he favored no doubt with the smiling
accommodation with which the good honest Gellert sings the praise
of poetry in the fable of the bee and the hen:

> Poems are useful: they can tell
> The truth by means of parable
> To those who are not very bright.
>
> (*Birth of Tragedy* 90)

It seems likely, though, that Joyce (being Joyce) has given us a pur-
posefully simplified version of a process that partakes of more complicated forms. Stephen, in any case, is destined to become confused
by poems more ambitious than this one and to dedicate himself,
famously and fatuously, to "encounter for the millionth time the
reality of experience and to forge in the smithy of [his] soul the
uncreated conscience of [his] race" (253).

That, perhaps—for better or worse, taken straight or with a dose
of corrosive Joycean irony—is really what a writer, if not any individual text, is "for."

In my dream of January 1, I received the wound of incoherence.
Who was the soldier who shot me? I can't say. Perhaps he was an
Iraqi, or a Viet Cong, or a Nazi, or a Brazilian, or a Martian; or
maybe he was an American, and the death he dealt me was an
instance of "friendly fire." Did he say "God" or "*Dieu*"? Why did he
kill me? In the dream, I had no more idea than I do now. The
incoherence there was also the incoherence of disenfranchisement.
I had no say in my own fate. I had no power. I was in the position of
a Kuwaiti civilian at the hands of an Iraqi invader, of an Iraqi civilian
under the bombs of the coalition—or of any thoughtful American
citizen watching the electro-mechanical titanium servomechanism
of the Reagan-Bush U.S. Army swing into action without my "authority." In my dream, as in reality when the war began, I was left in
a condition of numb and confused detachment. That is the face of

incoherence we must hate; that is the confusion we must fight against.

The wound of incoherence is obvious; but what is the gift of incoherence? Stephen Dedalus, in trying to draw his "thin thin line" around everything, is close to discovering it: Just as "he tried to think what a big thought that must be," he is possibly ready to grasp the genuine plurality of the world. It's not easy to think that way, and Stephen, as we have seen, suffers a failure of nerve; he draws back into nationalism, into language chauvinism. This is one of the points at which what I am calling incoherence ceases to be a gift and becomes a wound. There is nothing good about incoherence on the level of individual thinking; there is nothing good about it on the level of particular government policy. Its strength lies in imaginative application, where political incoherence is to anarchy as chaos science is to disorder. The challenge before us is to imagine our way toward a model of "body politic" that is malleable, permeable, a body organized not around a tyrant heart or brain but around, if anything, what chaos science calls a "strange attractor." What is needed is a body that can be heterogeneous and still live, one that can actually *occupy the same space* as other, similarly constructed bodies without doing any violence to them or to itself (for why should such a "body" be imagined as subject to the bounds of space and time?).

The Tudor monarch consists of two bodies with only one head. Its anatomy is deeply conservative, because in order to live it must maintain *this* shape and no other. It is hierarchal, insofar as one privileged class serves the function of brain, another of heart; those at the bottom are relegated to serve as muscle, sinew, bone, callus, toenail. It is also male and white (in spite of the fact that, for a certain definitive span, the monarch in the "Body natural" was significantly female) and does not appear ready to accept the full reality of those who say *Dieu*. Our "Body politic," by contrast, must be an utterly decentered shape-shifter, a protean body ready to express the structure of every mind and will it contains. It must be a body capable of being read backwards *and* forwards—and sideways, and diagonally in an infinite range of dimensions.

This is a politically harrowing idea because it is new, and it will initially appear, from the standpoint of the older politics, ungovernable; it is also an idea that *by definition* can never be perfectly accurately summarized or depicted (either literally or allegorically); a radical pluralism can never be exhausted in a single representation. That means it can never satisfy the older political craving—any more than a painting by Rothko, say, can satisfy the same aesthetic craving as one by Michelangelo. But what it promises is endless possibility, within the inevitability of the wholeness of humanity, and the means for interconnection beyond the "thin thin line" bounding language and nationality; it promises endless variety, endless revitalization.

"And because the Multitude naturally is not *One*," Hobbes writes, "but *Many*; they cannot be understood for one; but many Authors, of every thing their Representative faith, or doth in their name; Every man giving their common Represerter, Authority from himselfe" (220–21). Hobbes is not using the word "author" in quite our sense, but it suits my purpose to pretend that he is and to project from this passage the idea of a world in which every member is the author, not simply of his or her particular fate, but of the *shape of the whole*. Hobbes chooses to emphasize the "one man, or one Person" who represents and summarizes that multitude; America has already chosen to do the opposite. From this point, then, the United States—and every other such "body"—must have the courage to press the gift of incoherence as far as it will go and not to turn back at the first encounter of someone who says *Dieu* instead of *God*. The coherence of this definition of difference is precisely the danger.

Elias Canetti tells the following story in his essay "The Writer's Profession":

> By chance, I recently stumbled upon a jotting by an anonymous author, whose name I cannot give you simply because no one knows

it. This jotting bears the date August 23, 1939; that was a week before the outbreak of World War II. And it goes:

"But everything is over. If I were really a writer, I would have to
be able to prevent the war."

Canetti describes his initial impatience with this "jotting," his irritation with what he regarded as its pretentiousness—a well-founded
irritation with a Romantic privileging of art and hence of the artist.
But somehow he could not get it out of his mind:

The way it began was already odd: "But everything is over," an utterance of a complete and hopeless defeat in a time when victories
ought to begin. . . . In his despair at what *has* to happen now, [the
writer] accuses *himself*, not the true bearers of the responsibility,
whom he certainly knows precisely, for if he did not know them, he
would think differently about what is to come. Thus the source of
the original irritation remains one thing: his idea of what a writer
ought to be and the fact that he considered himself one until the
moment, when, with the outbreak of the war, everything collapsed
for him.

It is precisely this irrational claim to responsibility that gives me
pause to think and captivates me. One would also have to add that
words, deliberate and used over and over again, misused words, led
to this situation, in which the war became inevitable. If words can
do so much—why cannot words hinder it? It is not at all surprising
that a man who deals with words more than other people do will
also expect more of words and their effect. (237–39)

Part of the wound of incoherence is the fact that responsibility
(as both Nietzsche and Foucault acknowledge) becomes difficult if
not impossible to assign. But Canetti's anonymous author, unable to
accept that impossibility, does the only thing he can do: He takes on
the responsibility himself, no matter how irrational his gesture may
seem. This, I think, is a crucial clue, especially if we keep in mind
the Hobbesian idea that not only writers are authors in the process
of creating conscience; that the gift of incoherence can be realized

only through the discipline of a radical agnosticism applied on all fronts, and through the positive acceptance by *everyone* of the responsibility, the guilt and the grief, of not knowing the truth. This position is not based on despair; at the moment of despair, the moment when "everything collapsed for him," Canetti's author *ceases* to be an author. My argument is designed to reverse the current of that collapse. If everyone is an "author"—if there is not "one; but many Authors"—then conscience is rescued from collapse at the same moment we are all delivered from the blind grip of the Leviathan. What we all can know together is that we are together the authors of all we know. The authority of every human being herein becomes the agency of his or her unknowing. Such discipline is the first principle of a new craft of conscience. The peril of a moment such as the present, when a spurious and very dangerous coherence suddenly seems about to burst forth, is that the lesson of Canetti's author may be forgotten.

In a February 1, 1991, speech at Fort Stewart, Georgia, the first President Bush announced, "America has a new credibility . . . *what we say goes*." Our responsibility is to resist this sort of gesture, to refuse to "authorize" its substance and the temptation it holds out. But if language is the flesh of the body politic, and if, even against our vigilant protest, Bush's boast comes true, then he had better, we all had better, watch very carefully indeed *what* we say, and beware of *where* it goes.

Middlebury, Vermont, 1992

Postscript

The provinces of his body revolted.
—W. H. Auden

Like "'Sen-Sen,' Censorship, Obscenity, Secrecy," this essay addresses a situation that has mutated in such profound ways that revising or extending it to encompass the present is not possible.

When I read this piece in light of all that has passed since 2001, its concluding paragraph elides spookily into 2005; the first George Bush has become the second, the first Persian Gulf War has telescoped. A reader of this essay will, I suppose, either find it still relevant or not; for me, as with the essay on censorship, the argument still holds—and holds, if anything, all too well. What George W. Bush said in the weeks preceding our second invasion of Iraq has been analyzed ad infinitum by experts of virtually every stripe, and—particularly his accounts of Iraqi weapons of mass destruction and Iraqi complicity with Islamic terrorism—almost universally found untrue. The sources and motives for those untruths remain areas of speculation; in pragmatic terms, the untruths have scarcely seemed to matter.

The one thing that seems worth adding here is an extension of the central trope of the piece—the exploration of concrete consequences of cultural metaphors about the nature of the body politic. Though by now any illusion that our adventure in Iraq would be quick, clinical, and clean has disappeared, such was the original projection of the Bush government. Operation Shock and Awe would, it was said, anesthetize not only the Iraqi military but also the entire body politic; the incision would be painless, and the patient would thank us for it.

To reiterate, I originally observed that

the soldiers who carried out the combat in the Gulf region were projected more as physicians and medical technicians (albeit "heroic" ones) than as warriors; the media portrayal of the war smelled strongly of the operating room. There was a heavy odor of antiseptic and anaesthetic in the air, and the subject (whether patient or victim—and *was* the subject Kuwait, or the U.S.A.? Who was the main beneficiary of this "healing"?) was kept carefully under sterile wraps. Those of us in the spectator's seats beyond the plate glass arena window watched either with the helpless grief of relatives of the stricken (what's the prognosis? what will the specialists say?) or with the obsessive professional interest of the student surgeon (what happens next? can I learn that technique?).

This time around, the metaphor has operated even more powerfully and with more macabre detail: America the Robo-surgeon arrived to perform no less miraculous a surgery than a head transplant. Decapitated, the Iraqi body politic lay—and lies still—wracked by infection and fever, invaded by alien viruses, and kept on life support while the procedure has unfolded and then imploded.

There the matter lies as I write, and no one can foresee the outcome. The old head, in the guise of Saddam Hussein, goes on talking in its disembodied state, protesting the injustice of his situation—an opinion shared by no one. As to the new head, well, is there one? Robo-surgeon brought one along; but the Bush administration's replacement part, Ahmed Chalabi, quickly proved unviable.

What will become of this headless body? For Iraq, the main hope lies in the fact that the body politic is, as an organic body, fictive, albeit necessary. It can grow a new head, with Robo-surgeon's help or in his spite; it can mutate into a form of its own imagining; it can die and be reborn; it can simply die. It could become the Foucaultian "science fiction creature, all transparent protoplasm and veins of arcing blue light" cited above—a new thing, grown according to a new template. Or it could break apart into several nations—one Sunni, one Shiite, one Kurdish?—as centripetal forces native to its culture, which Hussein's regime controlled by brutalization, tear it apart. Daily the news brings conflicting information— an election, the formation of a government, the continual mutation of insurgency, hundreds of deaths every week. Whatever else may be said about this situation, it has not been precise, painless, or clean.

The best hope is that Iraq will regenerate itself and return from this peculiar beyond-death experience transformed for the better in the eyes of its own people. As for the United States, part of its job is to take a careful look at this surgical machine and see it for what it is. Deeply flawed and covered with blood, it has mangled the body it purported to be designed to heal. The second Bush administration and all its allies put their whole faith in this device; George W. Bush still talks the talk. What is inescapable for Americans is this: Robosurgeon is us, and Robosurgeon is, in terms of the necessary metaphor of the body politic, the cyborg child of Dr. Frankenstein. The hubris is the same: to make a living body, *ex nihilo* if that can be done, or if it can't (and *of course* it can't), then out of spare parts.

The Pentagon is dreaming of an all-robot army. If this idea seems outlandish, see "A New Model Army Soldier Rolls Closer to the Battlefield" in the February 16, 2005, issue of the *New York Times*. The idea is that war could at last be perfectly clean; our hardware can decimate their software, and the human cost (to us, at least) would be zero. This, perhaps, is how American will "spread democracy" in the future. And imagine the liberated peoples of the world then rushing out to embrace us shouting, "American robot! We love you, American machine!"

Athens, Georgia, 2005

"Christ, Start Again"

Robert Penn Warren, a Poet of the South?

In 1995, while living in Oregon, I was contacted by the editors of the Southern Review, founded by Robert Penn Warren when he was on the faculty at Louisiana State University. The university and the journal, I was told, were hosting a conference in honor of Warren, who had died in 1989. Would I be willing to come to Baton Rouge to deliver a paper on Mr. Warren's legacy?

I agreed immediately. Warren's work—the poetry especially—had been of great importance to me for a long time, and the opportunity to write about him was welcome. I spent a happy week or so thinking of the many very interesting facets of Warren's enormous body of work one might want to explore. Then I received a letter from LSU. I had an assignment: It was my job, I was told, to write about Warren as a southern poet.

My enthusiasm was immediately deflated. Although I understood the conference planners' strategy—my talk was to be paired with one by John Burt called "Robert Penn Warren as a Poet of New England," thus slyly bracketing Warren's flexibility and breadth—I was simply not interested in this subject. I felt typecast, for one thing: May a poet born in the South write only about "Southernness"?

Well, then, the perverse side of my nature answered, so be it; I will do the job and do it with a vengeance.

As I warmed to my task, I became, to my own surprise, grateful for the assignment. My relationship with "Southernness" has been lifelong and always agonistic; I had gone on record about it many times, in poetry as well as prose. Still, in this instance, thanks to what I saw at first as an imposition, I discovered that I had one more thing to say on the subject.

find it interesting and strange that I (of all people) should be called upon to explore the southernness (of all things) of Robert Penn Warren (of all poets). In the first place, Warren's southernness may at first glance appear—as it did to me when I first began thinking about this subject—so self-evident that any discussion along these lines would be tautological and therefore boring. It's certainly no problem, for anyone interested in doing so, to claim Warren as a southern poet. He may not be from the South, exactly, Kentucky being a border state (and I for one am not eager to get into any argument, especially with Kentuckians, over whether Kentucky is or is not southern in fact or in spirit), but his connection with the Fugitives and his founding of the *Southern Review* would appear immediately to certify him. One of the uninteresting ways to frame this discussion would be to rehearse those well-known facts and be done with it. Another would be to approach the poetry itself in a more or less statistical way and prove that 51.24 percent of Warren's poetry is of, for, or about the South. Yet another would be to put forward a number of themes, techniques, images, tonalities, or what have you as belonging specifically to southern poetry and go on to demonstrate that 51.24 percent of Warren's poetry possesses those qualities. Then we could spend all day arguing about whether those themes, techniques, images, tonalities, or what have you are really southern, or are only southern, and whether Warren's poetry really possesses them. This might be amusing, but my experience tells me that in the end it would get us nowhere.

My first impulse, in all honesty, is to wonder just how much the "Southernness" of Robert Penn Warren really matters. It's tempting simply to say that it doesn't matter at all and then pass on. But this response, no matter how much it appeals to me personally, is as bad as baldly saying "Of course Warren is Southern." The only intellectually decent way to solve the problem "Robert Penn Warren is/is not a Southern poet" is to define the terms. "What is the South?" is a familiar enough question at conferences on regional writing. But if we ask this question, are we not equally obliged to ask, "Well, but what is a poet?" And worst of all, "What is Robert Penn Warren?" I propose to answer all these questions in an alarmingly small number of words.

What Is the South?

Anyone who has spent time in the South has seen the bumper sticker that says, "American by Birth; Southern by the Grace of God." Therein lies one kind of definition of the South: an attitude.

Daniel Patrick Moynihan has recently made a telling distinction between *states* and *nations*, a state being a social organization to which one belongs by political fiat, a matter of boundaries, compromises, and laws, and a nation being a group larger than a tribe or a family, often an ethnicity, to which one belongs by birth. These definitions fit neatly in many parts of the world where one finds states comprised of many nations, or peoples who are strangely divided from one another by the artificial action of politics, or ethnic groups entirely deprived of homelands in which to create their own states. The history of the United States strangely subverts this formula: We call ourselves a nation that is comprised of many states, and we try as hard as we can, much of the time, to ignore the distinctions and the differences among the various peoples who comprise the realm. The famous bumper sticker cited above is a symptom of this subversion; Moynihan might revise it to read, "Die-cast American by accident; born Southern by the force of history."

American regions occupy a particularly anomalous position in this structure—neither states nor nations in fact, they are the ghosts of both. The word "region" is derived from the Latin word for king. American regions generally, and the South particularly—insofar as the South is the only American region I know of other than the regions of Utah and Texas that after the thirteen original colonies sorted themselves out still proposed to be separate countries—reflect the American desire to have everything both ways at once. We are, as the man says, "one nation, under God"; we are a vast plurality; we are a number of phantom kingdoms at odds with one another. Even within the peculiar American nesting of differences, the South contains its own rupture, the breach between the races—and though the whole earth suffers from racial tension, the South has made a mysticism of racial difference that is like no other: an attitude.

One may say with truth and justice that any region is simply a place wherein women and men carry on their lives, walking their distinctive walk, talking their idiosyncratic talk—but it is also true that the walk and the talk come from somewhere. That *somewhere* we can sum up under the heading of the single word *history*. A strongly discrete region like the South is the shade of a stillborn body politic, the wraith of a state that might have been, the itchy whisper of a realm of possibility terminated by circumstance, the echo of an alternate reality in the manner of *Star Trek* wherein things that might have been carry on a dim existence in spite of "actual" outcomes, in spite of circumstances, in spite of old bloodshed and battles lost, in spite in spite in spite. . . .

Regions are twitches in the amputated ghost limbs of history. We white southerners, as southerners, go on, like Hamlet, searching for the body of our murdered king, and mourning.

What Is a Poet?

Nobody knows what a poet is, and everyone does. The history of criticism is in no small part a junkyard of attempted definitions of the poet, the artist generally—each of which forms its own region in the life of writing, its own ghost kingdom. For present purposes, we can get off the hook pragmatically and decorously by using Warren's acute observations on the subject. In *Democracy and Poetry*, for instance, he asserts that "poetry—the work of the 'makers'—is a dynamic affirmation of, as well as the image of, the concept of the self," and that "the 'made thing'—the poem, the work of art—stands as a 'model' of the organized self." Warren, of course, is not so naive as to assume that the poet is a more or a less "organized self" than other people; often highly disorganized, he tells us, the poet projects *an image of the concept* of an ideal self out toward the future.

I repeat, for the sake of emphasis, that deep regression: an image of the concept of an ideal. As for the self itself, Warren maintains that it "is never to be found, but must be created, not the happy accident of passivity, but the product of a thousand actions, large and small, conscious or unconscious, performed not 'away from it all,' but in the face of 'it all,' for better or for worse." If all this begins to sound a little cozy, he goes on to tell us, "What poetry most significantly celebrates is the capacity of humanity to face the deep, dark inwardness of our nature and our fate." And of poets themselves, he says, "the artist may be regarded as the man [*or woman,* I would add] who cannot project outside himself the 'shadow' self, but must live with it." These ideas are provocative, Warren knew, precisely because they are contradictory. Together they point toward certain fundamental problems in American art, in the fabric of America itself, which lie in the basic paradox of the attempt to make not merely a state but a nation of utterly sovereign individuals.

This is the central problem not only of *Democracy and Poetry* but also of Warren's whole enterprise as a writer. Poetry, he says, is an enterprise "in which the doer pursues the doing as a projection of

his own nature upon objective nature, thereby discovering both the
law of the medium in which he chooses to work and his own nature." Whether or not this is universally true, Warren believed it.
Therefore, we can only look for the keys to his enterprise within the
enterprise itself.

What Is Robert Penn Warren?

Some years ago when I was in my middle thirties, a friend and fellow poet said to me, "Do you realize that if you wrote and published
a book a year for the next thirty years, you would not equal the output of Robert Penn Warren?"

It was the truth, and it was terrifying. Warren's output was enormous, even prodigal; whether or not we choose to speak of his gift,
his energy, his tenacity, his breadth, or his obsession, we are forced
to acknowledge that at least in sheer bulk it is beyond the reach of
most mere mortals. His work comprises a large and plural literary
region, a sort of kingdom. And insofar as Warren has now, for most
of us, gone to live entirely inside his books, he is the shadow monarch of all he chose to convey.

He was, as a matter of fact, a sort of king in life—or at least a
literary patriarch. I know a story—perhaps apocryphal but nonetheless true to the image—about Warren's giving a reading at a university where most of the audience consisted of undergraduates. Looking out at them, Warren reportedly said, "I'm delighted to see so
many young people in the audience tonight. I am the father you all
want to kill." Beyond some more or less indefinable moment in his
life and in his career, Robert Penn Warren became surely one of the
fathers.

Arguing against the American tendency to erase history, Warren
wrote in his essay "The Use of the Past" that "we live in a 'society
without fathers.'" He is talking about our ethos, not our sociology.
The patriarchs, to Warren, are the keepers of the lessons of the past,
as well as the past's enforcers; their mortmain is heavy, but it cannot

be safely ignored. America, he knows, has tried to do away with its patriarchs and all they stand for, and for good reason: That kind of hegemony is largely incommensurate with democracy. But, he believes, there is a stiff cost for this erasure, and the danger, as he sees it, is great.

If we combine this image of the patriarch with the image of the poet described above, we come up with a creature precariously balanced between past and future—a sort of emptiness (insofar as the self is no more than what we make of it) poised between a history that is leaden but necessary and a future that is an abyss. This is no new idea—it would have seemed downright homey to the Greeks—but Warren's rerendering of it is particularly harrowing. His universe is brutal and beautiful; his humanity is heroic but foolish and doomed. The past is unknowable but we have to know it; the future is unforeseeable but we have to create it. Warren readers, and especially Warren scholars, know all this very well. Warren makes it clear over and over again; in "The Use of the Past" he puts it this way: the fate of humanity

> is double, an outer and an inner fate, the world that the self is in, and the self that is a world. And more and more we see, painfully, that the two worlds are indissolubly linked and interpenetrating— mirror facing mirror, as it were—and more and more we see that one of the errors of the past, an error from which we must learn, has been to treat them as though each were in isolation.

This terrible and numinous universe limned with increasing clarity is Warren's own region, his kingdom. It's a hell of a place, but it's *his* place, and he makes it immense and dignified.

Precisely here I begin to discern the core of Warren's debt, and his attachment, to the South. A region with an attitude is inevitably going to be conservative in certain ways—it is tradition, after all, that makes the South the South, and makes it different from New England, say, which has its own distinct past and its own brand of conservatism. Marshall McLuhan somewhere points out that regions possess "an unconscious preference for a local and limited point of view." I would say, on the contrary, that the preference often is absolutely conscious. The region (not to say all its individuals) must go on living in the past and simultaneously in the virtual reality of the destroyed future of which it is the ghost. Otherwise, it ceases to be a region. At the same time, it must negotiate the actualities that surround and permeate it in any given present; otherwise it will be overwhelmed. So the New South negotiates with the Old South and with contemporary Manhattan, Paris, and Beijing. So too in the 1950s and '60s when I was growing up in Mississippi, the white South negotiated perforce with Washington and with its own disenfranchised African American population. Just at that juncture certain falsehoods in the sovereign mythos of the white South, and the "image of a concept of an ideal self," began to come apart at the seams. But the white South, of course, is far from the only South. The righteous demand, then as now, is that the old image of a concept give way to a new reality, a body politic capable of genuinely incorporating all its constituent citizens.

And Warren? How did this paradigm shift, if that is what it was, affect him, and how did he affect it? For if indeed he was in any way, shape, or form "southern," if his selfhood as a white male, a patriarch, was in any real way implicated with the fabric of twentieth-century southern culture, then events in the South just past midcentury must have had an impact on him and on his practice as a poet. If we can gauge the extent of that impact, we may begin to understand the southernness of his poetry.

What Is "Southern" about Warren's Poetry?

Warren's ambitious poem "Mortmain," which appeared in 1960 in his volume *You, Emperors, and Others*, has as its center the death of the narrator's (presumably Warren's own) father in 1955. The first section of the poem, subtitled "After Night Flight Son Reaches Bedside of Already Unconscious Father, Whose Right Hand Lifts in a

Spasmodic Gesture, as though Trying to Make Contact: 1955," begins this way:

> In Time's concatenation and
> Carnal conventicle, I,
> Arriving, being flung through dark and
> The abstract flight-grid of sky,
> Saw rising from the sweated sheet and
> Ruck of bedclothes ritualistically
> Reordered by the paid hand
> Of mercy—saw rising the hand—
>
> Christ, start again!

In his dying, the father is—predictably but nonetheless powerfully—identified with history, with guilt and debt, and also with the
human will. In his terror at that apparition, Warren's narrator delivers a characteristically Warrenesque response: "Christ, start again!"
As if starting again were possible here. And yet, paradoxically, it
turns out to be possible—through an unflinching rehearsal of the
father's history, and through it the son's. Mortmain, the dead hand
of the past, arrives to exact a debt that cannot be ignored but that can
eventually be worked off.

What is important about this moment is the impulse to *start
again*—not *ex nihilo* but as cognizant as possible of what has come
before: knowing that, in fact, the essence of starting again, even in
moments of profoundest crisis, is an honest and thorough taking
stock. The father's upraised hand becomes emblematic of that demand, that responsibility: "Like law, / The hand rose cold from History / To claw at a star in the black sky." And the narrator of the
poem must take his father—along with the demands of that "law,"
that "History," that "black sky"—completely into himself.

Years ago when I first began to engage Warren's poetry seriously,
the quality that most impressed itself on me was Warren's restless
insistence on transforming himself as a poet. In his first books, he
consolidates and masters the Fugitive style; "Bearded Oaks," for in-

stance, is in its way a perfect poem, albeit a relatively minor example of something prefabricated. Then in 1956—clearly a pivotal year for Warren—the magnificent book *Promises* blasted apart the relative purity of the early work (which had already been seriously disturbed earlier by "The Ballad of Billy Potts"), and from that point forward, Warren never ceased to hammer away at his own poetic assumptions and practices. Indeed, the most completely characteristic fact about Warren's poetry from *Promises* onward is its unwillingness to rest in any achieved style. Warren's poetry *is* a dialectic of change, of internal hammers and tongs and scalpels and sutures and wrecking balls and dynamite all trained inward, challenging its own generating and presiding ethos. Allegiance to what Warren calls "impure poetry" is symptomatic of that transformative restlessness; "Christ, start again!" is its battle cry.

But this internal obsession with a sort of mental urban renewal is not simply a stylistic concern, nor does it adhere merely to the practice of poetry. In "The Use of the Past," Warren declares "the will to change" the most fundamental of all American characteristics; put simply, he might say that the motto "Christ, start again!" could have been emblazoned on the bow of the *Mayflower* or over the doorway of the First Continental Congress. The selves of individuals, the selves of regions, the selves of nations—phantoms that they are, nowhere to be "discovered" or found, but only flickeringly created—are, in Warren's mythos, subject to a tortured ancient mariner kind of wandering; and painful and difficult as it is, this condition is necessary and even moral.

We have come to the crux of the argument, and so, before pressing to the end, I want to reiterate: So far we have "proved" that the South, like all American regions, is an attitude that is in turn a symptom of a historical amputation, a palpitation in a cultural ghost limb; we have "demonstrated" that a poet, from Warren's perspective at least, is the king of the ghosts, one of those who, importantly but paradoxically, is a purveyor of an infinite regress, the projector of an image of the concept of an ideal; and we have asserted that Warren, as he exists for us in his work, is himself a literary region—

which means, given this definition of *region*, that he is a zone containing representative ghosts foreshadowing the existence of other
ghosts, and is at the same time a patriarch among ghosts, however
unhappily so. As such, he might agree with the shade of Achilles in
the *Odyssey*, who

> would rather follow the plow as thrall to another
> man, one with no land allotted him and not much to live on,
> than be a king over all the perished dead.

Or would he? Achilles' speech might have an uncomfortable ring
in the ear of an attentive and historically conscious white southerner,
particular of Warren's generation. In southern terms, we know perfectly well who has perforce spent generations "following the plow
as thrall to another / man . . . with no land allotted him and not much
to live on," and know also perfectly well who has been king over everyone, living and dead alike. Warren himself wrote in 1930 in "The
Briar Patch," "Let the negro sit beneath his own vine and fig tree"—
a pallid expression of the old separate-but-equal doctrine that would
keep African Americans on the farm and "in their place" but would
at least make the "vine and fig tree" their own.

Christ, start again.

Warren's *Selected Poems, 1923–1975* contains, as one of the new
pieces in the book's opening section, "Can I See Arcturus from
Where I Stand," an uncomfortably revealing poem called "Old
Nigger on One-Mule Cart Encountered Late at Night When Driving
Home from Party in the Back Country." The poem's narrator, a
white man who is doing the driving described in its title, drunk and
distracted by a sexual memory of a woman with whom he has just
been dancing, takes a curve too fast and finds himself confronted by
the title's other character, discovered in the headlights.

> On the fool-nigger ass-hole wrong side of
> The road, naturally. And the mule head
> Thrusts at us, and ablaze in our headlights,

Outstaring from primal bone-blankness and the arrogant
Stupidity of skull snatched there
From darkness and the saurian stew of pre-Time,
For an instant—the eyes,
They blaze from the incandescent magma
Of mule-brain. Thus mule-eyes. Then
Man-eyes, not blazing, white-bulging
In black face, in black night, and man-mouth
Wide open, the shape of an O, for the scream
That does not come. Even now,
That much in my imagination, I see.

The narrator calls the black man and his mule cart a "death trap," but it's easy to see who constitutes the real danger here: The narrator, one of the profligate kings of the earth, implicitly confident in his ownership of everything and his freedom to do simply anything, is plainly out of control. He goes home, indulges in "the one last drink" and a "sweat-grapple in darkness" with an unidentified partner, but wakes again with the image of the mule-driver's face in his mind and attempts a poem, which turns out badly:

And remember
Now only the couplet of what
Had aimed to be—Jesus Christ—a sonnet:

One of those who gather junk and wire to use
For purposes that we cannot peruse. . . .

As I said, Jesus Christ.

In this poem, we can discern one pole of Warren's southernness: He knows the peculiarly southern version of racism and can portray its psychology to perfection. He also understands how to project the dangers entailed in the kind of mental power this poem's narrator assumes. It is not merely a reflexive or overfastidious political correctness that leads a careful reader to worry about the profound selfishness the poem's central character exhibits: He is not only the author of a badly failed sonnet, he is a danger to himself and to others. Warren's poem knows this perfectly well, and demonstrates it in another characteristic "Christ, start again!" transition:

> Moved on through the years. Am here. Another
> Land, another love.

Between 1930—the year of "The Briar Patch"—and 1956, when he published a strange and fascinating essay called "Segregation: The Inner Conflict in the South," Warren traveled great distances, physically as well as mentally. In "Segregation," Warren travels south as an expatriate, what he calls an "outlander" or a "corrupted native," to talk to southerners about race relations. Time and space will not here permit a full consideration of this essay and all its ramifications. Suffice it to say that it provides evidence that a powerful "start again," or more than one, had taken place since the complacencies of "The Briar Patch." Interviewing himself at the end of the essay, Warren presents the following Q & A:

> Q. Are you for desegregation?
> A. *Yes.*

This emphatic "yes" demonstrates that a universe has intervened between 1930 and 1956. "Segregation" is full of contempt for those who evince a "preference for a local and limited point of view," whether conscious or unconscious. Likewise, in the "One-Mule Cart" poem, the narrator, who has "moved on through the years," has grown in humanity and understanding. Imaginatively, he revisits the black man, whom he now mentally locates

> By a bare field that years pale in starlight, the askew
> Shack. He arrives there. Unhitches the mule.
> Stakes it out. Between cart and shack,
> Pauses to make water, and while
> The soft, plopping sound in deep dust continues, his face
> Is lifted into starlight, calm as prayer.

The poem then concludes with a prayer to that image of a concept of a man:

> Brother, Rebuker, my Philosopher past all
> Casuistry, will you be with me when
> I arrive and leave my own cart of junk
> Unfended from the storm of starlight and
> The howl, like wind, of the world's monstrous blessedness,
> To enter, by a bare field, a shack unlit?
> Entering into that darkness to fumble
> My way to a place to lie down, but holding,
> I trust, in my hand, a name—
> Like a shell, a dry flower, a worn stone, a toy—merely
> A hard-won something that may, while Time
> Backward unblooms out of time toward peace, utter
> Its small, sober, and inestimable
> Glow, trophy of truth.
>
> Can I see Arcturus from where I stand?

For all the "improvement" in the thought of the narrator over the undivulged distances of the leap at the center of the poem, this text's projection of what we have come in such facile fashion to label "the other" presents problems. The man at the end of the poem, after all, is unreal—only a memory construct, arguably a sentimentalized one, invoked to aggrandize the narrator, to redeem him. The real man on the real mule cart remains as unknown and unrepresented as ever. Most convincing here is the placement of both characters against a stark and inhuman background—winter night, cold, the black abyssal starry icy sky. This comes out of the South, but is not the South. It is memory. It is guilt remembered.

I love Warren's work, but I dislike this poem—very likely because I discover in it too many painful traces of my own experience as a white southerner. I wish not only that it had never been written, but that its materials and its psychology, the situations and emotions it describes, had never existed, never been imagined. Nevertheless, I find it eminently believable. Once racism has raised its cold hand and laid its mortmain on any mind, it can never be eradicated. No one escapes it; one can only resist it.

The most potent resistance this particular poem presents lies in its Wordsworthian abstracting force. At the end of the poem, the backdrop is no longer an American or even a human region; it is the vacuum of the night sky, the cosmos, against which our human profiles dim and flicker, ectoplasmic. Whatever Arcturus may be, it is not located in Tennessee.

"If," as Warren wrote in "Segregation," "the South is really able to face up to itself and its situation, it may achieve identity, moral identity. Then in a country where moral identity is hard to come by, the South, because it has had to deal concretely with a moral problem, may offer some leadership. And we need any we can get." One implication of this passage is that the South—like other places—has tended to project and promote "immoral" identity, false images of selfhood, false consciousness. The drunk and dangerous narrator of the "One-Mule Cart" poem is a dramatization of that way of being. What the South—and America, and humanity—ought to claim in Warren is the dire and bitter and sometimes thoroughly unappealing honesty of his struggle.

In one of Warren's finest poems—"Homage to Emerson on Night Flight to New York"—the narrator looks out the window of a plane as it approaches landing and thinks, "I have friends down there, and their lives have strange shapes / Like eggs spattered on the kitchen floor. Their lives shine / Like oil-slicks on dark water. I love them, I think." This is no self-serving projection of otherness; it is an acknowledgment of the utter strangeness of all our lives. Insofar as a region seeks to define itself in a complacency of sameness, it denies the simplest truths about our nature; Warren offers the South the opportunity to claim its own human weirdness. We all ought to be eager to accept this offer.

That said, I will also contradict myself by contending that the

desire to claim a writer for a region pure and simple seems to me
sadly misplaced and also dangerous. More than a waste of time, it
represents a failure of imagination. Why would we want to crystallize Warren in the South like a fly in amber? The perilousness of any
such attempt lies precisely in the extent to which it denies and falsi-
fies his struggle against his own worst tendencies—the "Christ,
start again!" for which we ought to value him most of all.

The Mechanical Muse

The distance between music and language—the impossibility of describing music in words, of echoing words in music, the incommensurability of phoneme and tone—is both obvious and notorious, but so is their inextricability. No one has expressed this paradox better than Nietzsche, two quotes from whom will serve to chart out this treacherous territory:

> Imagine, after all preconditions, what an undertaking it must be
> to write music for a poem, that is, to wish to illustrate a poem by
> means of music, in order to secure a conceptual language for music
> in this way. What an inverted world! An undertaking that strikes one
> as if a son desired to beget his father! (Fragment, Spring 1871)

> [T]he most important phenomenon of all ancient lyric poetry: they
> took for granted *the union*, indeed the *identity* of the lyrist with the
> musician. Compared with this, our modern lyric poetry seems like
> the statue of a god without a head. (*The Birth of Tragedy*, 1872)

Anyone who has ever thought seriously about this relationship—much less been a practitioner whose work leads into this abyss—will recognize the problem. Music and language are as distinct, and as linked, as the lobes of the brain. Talk about it for a while, and shortly you will begin to sound mystical.

It would be interesting to know how many poets of our generation are or have been musicians—whether practicing, failing, dabbling, wannabe, or ex—and how that proportion compares with the population at large. A survey might well reveal, as with a famous "statistic" about suicide, that even more dentists have tried it than poets. Ours is a music-saturated culture in which a certain kind of musician enjoys special status in the popular imagination. So many garages have begat so many decibels, so many high schools have encouraged so many out-of-tune choruses of trombone and violin, that you'd think *everybody* had been in a band at one time or another. Perhaps the attempt is an American rite of passage.

However mundane the idea of a middle-aged male such as myself still caught in the dream of performance (I don't say *stardom* because I honestly was never quite *that* stupid), a mystery remains here. Whether we are considering the Homeric hymns or the latest recording of Robert Bly in the guise of a damsel with a dulcimer, the poet is considered the musician of writers—which means that, however inexpressible the relation may be, the poet's job is to reassemble what so often presents itself as a broken primal unity.

For poets who write primarily for the page, the problem is compounded by the insistent silence of texts. The text is the instrument such a poet plays; and it is notoriously difficult to master precisely because it is so transparent. Too often, models of the poet's work project an unmediated voice "singing" to an audience. "Who touches this book touches a man," Whitman beautifully and falsely wrote. Whitman was one of the greatest virtuosi of the page we have ever had, and though he had his reasons for doing so, he insulted his instrument by pretending it did not exist—as if a bagpiper should pretend that all those caterwauls were coming from his own throat.

In the case of the poem on the page, one then thinks, "What caterwauls?" The page is as silent as the grave—which is the true motivation behind Whitman's resurrection of the book. Named, as we know, for "the beautiful uncut hair of graves," the barbaric yawp of *Leaves of Grass* is thus rendered a kind of Christ. However splendid it may be otherwise, from the perspective of the page, the poor, insulted instrument, this is a gross mystification.

The counterstory I have to tell concerns the instrument—the thing itself as thing—and its neglect not only in our poetics but also in the "higher" forms of our musicology.

The scene is a run-down band room in a run-down school in east central Mississippi; the year is 1959. We are gathered here, we offspring and our parents, because of the children's musical aptitude, demonstrated by a mastery achieved the previous year on a cheap plastic recorder known as the Flutophone, an instrument capable of producing little more than a thin whistle that, when multiplied in the inept hands of forty or so eight-year-olds, becomes a kind of teakettle of horror. But somehow we are chosen, and here we are, confronted by a roomful of brand-new band instruments lying in state in their cases: clarinets, trombones, trumpets, flutes, French horns, drums, and the one I am about to choose: the saxophone.

This is immediately a mysterious moment. Do not underestimate my ignorance at the age of nine. I grew up on a farm in that distant Jim Crow Mississippi, a place where art generally and music particularly were not much noticed, no matter how many musicians have been engendered there. Music arrived on the radio, of course, and tinkled along in the background of our doings; it lived too in church. Guitars, pianos, pump organs, drums—these instruments were familiar, both to the eye and to the ear. But saxophones? At the age of nine, had I ever even *heard* one? Surely I must have registered some of those fat and bluesy rides from old rock-and-rollers (Ace Cannon!) on the radio, but I had never given it any thought. My exposure to the saxophone as a *voice* was certainly minimal or nonexistent. But there in the band room I fall suddenly and deeply in love with the saxophone as a *thing*.

It lies there in its case, a gold and nickel glitter. It *smells* wonderful—new instruments, or more likely their cases, have a terrific aroma, like new cars. I walk around the room with my parents once in an obligatory kind of way: There the other instruments lie, in *their* cases, all a gold and nickel glitter, all smelling wonderful. But it is the saxophone I want, a student model alto, the Conn Director, its case dark blue with a powder-blue interior. I have never given a moment's thought to saxophones, but I take one look at it and the other instruments vanish. I am in love.

Why the saxophone? Honestly, I have no idea. Why do you love your lover? What lightning strikes you? Somehow, however dimly, I know that this is the instrument and that this knowledge and this feeling are important.

The fact is, the instrument—the object, the thing—cast a kind of spell on me. In the months that followed, I received only the barest instruction; our benighted little school had only one overworked band director for everyone, grades one through twelve. But I wanted this, and I worked at it. My fascination could not have been with the music I wanted to play, because I did not know what that was, nor with the sound of the instrument, because I did not know what that should be. I was attending to, and being taught by, the instrument itself. It was literally years before I began to study *music* with any real attention, and when I did, it was only because my horn insisted on it. It also took years for me to learn to generalize about my obsession, and I began to do so only when my band director advised me to trade the Conn for a better one—then I saw that it was not *that* saxophone but *all* saxophones I loved. Music as such, like agape, waited at a distance with its face half turned away.

If this dynamic sounds compulsive-obsessive or fetishistic, so perhaps are all children, so certainly is all art. Because my saxophone was gold and marvelously curved and metallic and somehow distant, I came into its presence with respect. A farm boy in subtropical Mississippi, I would not approach the instrument when I was dirty (as I often was) or wearing short pants. I had to be bathed and dressed appropriately; otherwise, I was unworthy. I felt unworthy in any case. The instrument chastised and then chastened me. I would practice in the back hallway—both for privacy and for the acoustics—where it so happened my mother's full-length mirror was attached to the bedroom door; I *watched* myself as I played, and knew that I must stand up straight in the presence of my beloved. My posture had to be commensurate with my emotions; otherwise, I was unclean and felt rejected. A particular stance was appropriate; a self-consciousness and an ethos were necessary.

I did not have this language, but I felt these things, which was extraordinary. Nothing else in my life taught me that I must have a stance, that an ethos was necessary. I learned decorum; I learned humility; I learned ecstasy. I also began, slowly, to learn music, which in the end demanded an even more precise stance, an even more arduous ethos. At the age of nine, a white farm boy in the heart of the Jim Crow South, I could not have approached that power unmediated.

Poetry stood even farther off; but years later, when I discovered it for myself, I had already learned important lessons. I had learned to be something I scarcely know how I could have learned otherwise: an artist, to be which means, in sum, to give yourself up to something and let it chasten and shape you, so that you may in the fullness of time turn back with humility and love and shape it in return.

Every art and every artist has its instrument, for there is no unmediated art. And every artist-in-progress has teachers, whether human, book, canvas, stone, or metal ones. In the place I found myself, there were no artists, no human teachers. The very word, had you tried to apply it to me at the age of nine or ten or eleven, would have baffled and embarrassed me. Fortunately, the instrument itself teaches; the instrument, like the beloved, becomes a second self, a second nature.

In the end, the mystery remains a mystery—one for which I am almost abjectly grateful. The saxophone taught me, by inclination an inarticulate slumper, to stand up straight and to try to speak. Later it taught me the value of a certain destructive connection to tradition, but that was after it led me to music, and thence to jazz, a process that took years. What is most important in this relation is that the saxophone, the thing itself, was my first passion, and my first exemplar. I am terrified to think what I might have become without it, because it led me into my own life in the 1960s in a way that no other influence in my immediate world could have done.

Why the saxophone? I ask again, as I have asked so many times before. All I can say with certainty is that something about it suits me. Perhaps it is the ridiculous complexity of the object. Compared to the more elegant and mysterious-looking trumpet or French horn, the saxophone is a Rube Goldberg contraption; invented in the Machine Age, it is the apotheosis of the musical instrument as machine—as the violin is the apotheosis of musical instrument as furniture or the pipe organ that of the musical instrument as architecture, the trumpet that of the musical instrument as plumbing. I can look at certain of my poems in that light and see a similarity: complex machination, out of which issues a voice that is *almost* human.

In the end, the question does not matter. In other circumstances, I might be asking "Why the bagpipe?" or "Why the kalimba?" with equal gratitude. What signifies is that, almost miraculously, I began to learn the discipline of instruments in the presence of a curved metal pipe; I began to be an artist under the tutelage of a golden machine. If this sounds like the story of a primitive who gains power and knowledge from a collection of soda cans and Styrofoam washed up on a beach, so be it; Mississippi was my island of exile, and I was its Caliban. It is a tribute to music—incarnated in a glorious, cheap saxophone—that it could find me even there.

Works Cited

An Audience

Jarrell, Randall. "The Obscurity of the Poet." In *Poetry and the Age*. New York: Ecco Press, 1980.

Ong, Walter. "The Writer's Audience Is Always a Fiction." In *Interfaces of the Word: Studies in the Evolution of Consciousness and Culture*. Ithaca, N.Y.: Cornell University Press, 1977.

Laughed Off: Canon, *Kharakter*, and the Dismissal of Vachel Lindsay

Carpenter, Humphrey. *A Serious Character: The Life of Ezra Pound*. Boston: Houghton Mifflin, 1988.

Damon, S. Foster. *Amy Lowell: A Chronicle*. Boston: Houghton Mifflin, 1935.

Eastman, Max. "American Ideals of Poetry, I." *New Republic* 16:202 (September 14, 1918): 190–92.

———. "American Ideals of Poetry, II." *New Republic* 16:203 (September 21, 1918): 222–25.

Eliot, T. S. *The Letters of T. S. Eliot*. Vol. 1, *1898–1922*. Edited by Valerie Eliot. San Diego: Harcourt Brace Jovanovich, 1988.

Engler, Balz. "Vachel Lindsay and the Town of American Visions." *Literature in Performance* 3:1 (November 1982): 27–34.

Ginsberg, Allen. "Improvisation in Beijing." In *Cosmopolitan Greetings: Poems, 1986–1992*. New York: HarperCollins, 1994.

Gray, Paul H. "Performance and the Bardic Ambition of Vachel Lindsay." *Text and Performance Quarterly* 9:3 (July 1989): 216–23.

Hardwick, Elizabeth. "Wind from the Prairie." *New York Review of Books* 38:20 (September 1991): 9–16.

Heymann, C. David. *American Aristocracy: The Lives and Times of James Russell, Amy, and Robert Lowell*. New York: Dodd, Mead, 1979.

Lindsay, Vachel. *Collected Poems*, with an introduction by Lindsay, "Adventures Preaching Hieroglyphic Sermons" (xvii–xlviii). 1925. Revised and illustrated edition, New York: Macmillan, 1934.

———. *General William Booth Enters into Heaven and Other Poems*. Introduction by Robert Nichols. New York: M. Kennerley, 1919.

———. *Letters of Vachel Lindsay*. Edited by Marc Chénetier. New York: Burt Franklin, 1979.

———. *The Poetry of Vachel Lindsay: Complete and with Lindsay's Drawings*. Edited by Dennis Camp. 2 vols. Peoria, Ill.: Spoon River Poetry Press, 1984.

———. *The Prose of Vachel Lindsay*. Edited by Dennis Camp. Peoria, Ill.: Spoon River Poetry Press, 1988.

———. "Walt Whitman." In "Views of American Poetry," special supplement, *New Republic* (December 5, 1923): 3–5.

Lowell, Amy. *A Critical Fable*. Boston: Houghton Mifflin, 1924.

———. *Pictures of the Floating World*. New York: Macmillan, 1919.

———. *Selected Poems of Amy Lowell*. Edited by John Livingston Lowes. Boston: Houghton Mifflin, 1928.

———. *Tendencies in Modern American Poetry*. New York: Macmillan, 1917.

Masters, Edgar Lee. *Vachel Lindsay: A Poet in America*. New York: Scribner's, 1935.

Monroe, Harriet. *A Poet's Life*. New York: Macmillan, 1938.

———. *Poets and Their Art*. New York: Macmillan, 1926.

Morrison, Toni. *Playing in the Dark: Whiteness and the Literary Imagination*. Cambridge, Mass.: Harvard University Press, 1992.

Nelson, Cary. *Repression and Recovery: Modern American Poetry and the Politics of Cultural Memory, 1910–1945*. Madison: University of Wisconsin Press, 1989.

Patterson, William Morrison. *The Rhythm of Prose: An Experimental Investigation of Individual Difference in the Sense of Rhythm*. New York: Columbia University Press, 1916.

Perkins, David. *A History of Modern Poetry*. Vol. 1, *From the 1890s to the High Modernist Mode*. Cambridge, Mass.: Harvard University Press, 1976.

Pound, Ezra. "Patria Mea." In *Selected Prose, 1909–1965*. Edited by William Cookson. New York: New Directions, 1973.

———. *The Spirit of Romance*. 1952. Reprint, New York: New Directions, 1968.

————. "What I Feel about Walt Whitman." In *Selected Prose, 1909–1965*. Edited by William Cookson. New York: New Directions, 1973.

Rampersad, Arnold. *The Life of Langston Hughes*. Vol. 1, *1902–1941, I, Too, Sing America*. New York: Oxford University Press, 1986.

R. S. B., "Sincerity in the Making." *New Republic* 1:5 (December 5, 1914): 26–27.

Ruggles, Eleanor. *The West-Going Heart: A Life of Vachel Lindsay*. New York: Norton, 1959.

Spears, Monroe K. *Dionysus and the City: Modernism in Twentieth-Century Poetry*. New York: Oxford University Press, 1970.

Whitman, Walt. *Democratic Vistas, and Other Papers*. London: Walter Scott, 1970.

Woolf, Virginia. "An American Poet." In *The Essays of Virginia Woolf*. Vol. 3: *1919–1924*. Edited by Andrew McNeillie. San Diego: Harcourt Brace Jovanovich, 1986.

————. *Mr. Bennett and Mrs. Brown*. Norwood, Pa.: Norwood Editions, 1978.

————. *Mrs. Dalloway*. With a foreword by Maureen Howard. New York: Harcourt Brace Jovanovich, 1981.

"Sen-Sen," Censorship, Obscenity, Secrecy: Slapping the Face of the Body Politic

"Artistic Freedom: Our American Heritage." Document issued from a Washington D.C. meeting of artists and arts organizations, May 30, 1990. Obtained from the Coalition of Writers' Organizations.

Bloom, Harold. *Ruin the Sacred Truths*. Cambridge, Mass.: Harvard University Press, 1989.

Blotner, Joseph. *Faulkner: A Biography*. New York: Random House, 1984.

Campbell, Ewing. Privacy Form. Sent to the office of Rep. Joe Barton, March 25, 1990.

————. "The 'Arts Ayatollahs' Holding Freedoms Hostage." *Houston Chronicle*, June 6, 1990.

————. "Sister Love." *New England Review and Bread Loaf Quarterly* 11:1 (Autumn 1988).

Conn, Charis W. Letter to Ewing Campbell, Feb. 8, 1989.

Fenza, D. W. "Coalition of Writers' Organizations Mobilizes for Censorship Battle." *AWP Chronicle* 22:5 (March/April 1990).

Frohnmayer, John. Letter to Rep. Joe Barton, May 14, 1990.

Grant, Lyman. "Introduction." In *New Growth: Contemporary Short Stories by Texas Writers*. San Antonio, Tex.: Corona, 1989.

Helms, Jesse. Letter to Charles A. Bowsher, Comptroller General, March 6, 1990.

———. Letter to Michael Chitwood, May 16, 1990.

Joyce, James. *Ulysses: The Corrected Text.* Edited by Hans Walter Gabler with Wolfhard Steppe and Claus Melchior. New York: Random House, 1986.

Kassebaum, Nancy Landon. Letter to David Levi Strauss, May 16, 1990.

Milligan, Bryce. "*New Growth* Rejuvenates Texas Short Stories." *San Antonio Light,* October 8, 1989.

Oliphant, Dave. "Limited Growth." *Texas Observer,* April 20, 1990.

Pinsky, Robert. *Poetry and the World.* New York: Ecco, 1988.

"Responding to Censorship: New Coalition Enters Turmoil in the Arts." *AWP Chronicle* 22:4 (February 1990).

Rushdie, Salman. Editorial. *New York Times,* February 15, 1989.

———. *The Satanic Verses.* London: Viking, 1988.

Safire, William. "Stop Subsidizing the Arts." *New York Times,* May 18, 1990.

Vendler, Helen. "Feminism and Literature." *New York Review of Books* 37:9 (May 31, 1990).

Inside the Avalanche

Foucault, Michel. *The Archaeology of Knowledge.* Translated by A. M. Sheridan Smith. New York: Pantheon Books, 1972.

Milosz, Czeslaw. "Ars Poetica." In *The Collected Poems, 1931–1987.* New York: Ecco Press, 1988.

Rich, Adrienne. *The Fact of a Doorframe: Poems Selected and New, 1950–1984.* New York: W. W. Norton, 1984.

Unterecker, John. *Voyager: A Life of Hart Crane.* New York: Farrar, Straus and Giroux, 1969.

Revenge of the American Leviathan

Axton, Marie. *The Queen's Two Bodies: Drama and the Elizabethan Succession.* London: Royal Historical Society, 1977.

Beard, Charles A., and William Beard. *The American Leviathan.* New York: Macmillan, 1930.

Bush, George. Speech delivered at Fort Stewart, Ga. CNN, February 1, 1991.

Canetti, Elias. "The Writer's Profession." In *The Conscience of the Word.* Translated by Joachim Neugroschel. New York: Seabury, 1979.

Collingwood, R. G. *The New Leviathan.* Oxford: Clarendon, 1942.

Foucault, Michel. *The History of Sexuality.* Vol. 1: *An Introduction.* Translated by Robert Hurley. New York: Vintage, 1980.

Hedges, Chris. "In Growing Disarray, Iraqis Fight Iraqis." *New York Times*, March 10, 1991, 1, 14.

Hobbes, Thomas. *Leviathan*. Edited and with an introduction by C. B. Macpherson. Baltimore: Penguin, 1968.

Jameson, Frederic. *Postmodernism: The Cultural Logic of Late Capitalism*. Durham: Duke University Press, 1991.

Joyce, James. *Portrait of the Artist as a Young Man*. New York: Penguin, 1976.

Kantorowicz, Ernst H. *The King's Two Bodies: A Study in Mediaeval Political Theology*. Princeton, N.J.: Princeton University Press, 1957.

Margulis, Lynn. "Speculation on Speculation." In *Speculations*. Edited by John Brockman. New York: Prentice Hall, 1990.

Nietzsche, Frederick. *The Birth of Tragedy and The Case of Wagner*. Translated by Walter Kaufmann. New York: Vintage, 1967.

———. *Twilight of the Idols*. Translated by Walter Kaufmann. The Portable Nietzsche. New York: Viking, 1968.

Pye, Christopher. "The Sovereign, the Theater, and the Kingdome of Darknesse: Hobbes and the Spectacle of Power." In *Representing the English Renaissance*. Edited by Stephen Greenblatt. Berkeley: University of California Press, 1988.

Scarry, Elaine. *The Body in Pain*. New York: Oxford, 1985.

Schmitt, Eric. "Unforeseen Problems in Air War Forced Allies to Improvise Tactics." *New York Times*, March 10, 1991, 1, 16.

"Christ, Start Again": Robert Penn Warren, a Poet of the South?

Homer. *The Odyssey*. Translated by Richmond Lattimore. New York: Harper and Row, 1967.

Moynihan, Daniel P. *Pandaemonium: Ethnicity in International Politics*. New York: Oxford University Press, 1993.

Warren, Robert Penn. "The Briar Patch." In *I'll Take My Stand: The South and the Agrarian Tradition, by Twelve Southerners*. New York: Harper, 1930.

———. *Democracy and Poetry*. Cambridge, Mass.: Harvard University Press, 1975.

———. "Homage to Emerson on Night Flight to New York." In *Selected Poems 1923–1975*. New York: Random House, 1976.

———. "Mortmain." In *You, Emperors, and Others*. New York: Random House, 1960.

———. "Old Nigger on One-Mule Cart Encountered Late at Night When Driving Home from Party in the Back Country." In *Selected Poems 1923–1975*. New York: Random House, 1976.

———. *Segregation: The Inner Conflict in the South.* New York: Random House, 1956.
———. "The Use of the Past." In *New and Selected Essays.* New York: Random House, 1989.

The Mechanical Muse

Nietzsche, Frederick. *The Birth of Tragedy and Other Writings.* Edited by Raymond Geuss and Ronald Speirs. Translated by Ronald Speirs. Cambridge: Cambridge University Press, 1999.
———. "On Music and Words." Quoted in David B. Allison, "On Nietzsche's 'On Music and Words.'" *New Nietzsche Studies* 1, no. 1/2 (Fall 1996): 5–41.
Whitman, Walt. *Leaves of Grass.* 1855 ed. Edited by Justin Kaplan. New York: Library of America, 1984.

Index

The Life of Poetry
Poets on Their Art and Craft

Carl Dennis
Poetry as Persuasion

T. R. Hummer
The Muse in the Machine:
Essays on Poetry and the Anatomy
of the Body Politic

Paul Mariani
God and the Imagination:
On Poets, Poetry, and the Ineffable

Gregory Orr
Poetry as Survival

Michael Ryan
A Difficult Grace:
On Poets, Poetry, and Writing

Sherod Santos
A Poetry of Two Minds

Ellen Bryant Voigt
The Flexible Lyric